She is a Spirit Now

Farzaneh Ghadirian

SHE IS A SPIRIT NOW/Farzaneh Ghadirian 1st Edition
ISBN 978-0-6456495-1-2

Contents

I dedicate this book to my mother and father.
I love them both equally.

Mum, thank you for leading me
on the spiritual journey of enlightenment.

This book is broken into two parts. The first part is about how I overcame a life filled with grieving and suffering by healing in just three nights. The pain of overcoming me was difficult, but I am finally free.

The second part is about how I halted the cycle of pain and suffering that had become my family's legacy.

The book itself is a memoir about inner transformation and self-improvement, about self-growth and spiritual awakening. My methodology was derived from the philosophies of spiritual teachers such as Alan Watts, Eckhart Tolle, Dr. Wayne Dyer, and Dr. Joe Dispenza, as well as through the study of Taoism and applying its teachings in the pursuit of a better life.

Part One

CHAPTER ONE

We Freed Each Other

Farzaneh Ghadirian

In April 2021, I was given the news that my mother had passed away. I paused in the corner of the kitchen, lying on the bench, not knowing how to feel anymore. Years of pent-up emotions of agony and resentment suddenly vanished from my shoulders. Deep down, I was happy for my mother: she was free. Free from her physical form and from her pain and suffering. I pretended I was more upset or sad about her passing. While I did cry when my husband and children came home, I felt numb inside. It reminded me of what it's like when one is in horrible, unrelenting physical pain, and then being given an anesthetic and feeling completely paralyzed. I could see now. There was a massive fog lifted from my eyes and an unbearable pain moved out like dust in the air. I felt relieved but sad, happy but sorrowful.

I dug into every social media platform to try to understand what I was feeling. I needed to hear from people, to feel their love and support in that difficult time. I experienced lots of emotions that I could not name or identify. I slept soundly that night and went back to work the very next day because I didn't feel the need to take time off to grieve. There was nothing to grieve. After all, I knew that day would come, and I had been preparing myself in the last few years to hear that news and not show any emotion about it. I wanted to feel empowered and in control. I wanted to prove to myself that I was fine and that losing a parent with whom I never connected was not a big deal at all.

The next day, I went to work and told my colleagues that my mother had passed away. I was showered with love and words of condolence. My husband was very supportive during that time. He kept checking on me, making sure I was okay. I received so many flowers to my house, sent from everyone who heard the news.

But despite this outpouring of sympathy, something was still missing. The heavy feeling in my chest was still messing with my head. I kept asking myself, "Now what?" Those who knew my personal story kept checking on me, noting the fact that I did not appear angry or devastated by my mother's death. They knew what I had gone through with her. They were surprised that her passing did not lead to another episode of sadness and resentment in me as it had when she had been alive. I didn't know what it was with me either, but I could only surmise that the many extensive counselling sessions with my psychologist had helped prepare me for the day I would lose her.

I attended her virtual funeral with a million questions in my head. I felt light, not heavy-hearted, yet still a bit broken inside. As usual, I tricked myself into believing that I was okay and that I was stronger than what comes my way. Things didn't go as I had expected. Watching the funeral left me in pain and agony. As most of my siblings were living away from our hometown, my eldest brother ordered standing funeral sprays from everyone...except me. As the standing sprays were arranged into a display at the burial site and a cameraperson filmed the flower arrangements, I kept looking but didn't find one with my name on it. I contacted my niece late that night, and she confirmed that my brother intentionally didn't order any flowers in my name.

Something happened to me in that moment. My body started shaking, and I began wailing. I saw myself alone at my dad's funeral all over again, and a deep sense of fear and anxiety rushed through me. My husband heard me sobbing and hurried to the bedroom where he held me tight in his arms to comfort me. I told my husband I felt so alone and scared, and I didn't know what would happen after tonight. He gently calmed me down, repeating my name several times. Looking into my eyes, he told me I was not going to be alone this time. He was with me. I stared at him, suddenly realising I was no longer a thirteen-year-old girl who had lost her father. I was not going to be alone this time. I had my husband and my children with me.

I was relieved, yet still heartbroken about how my brother wanted to make me feel. When I went to sleep that night, I saw my mother in my dreams. She was beautiful and well-dressed. There were no hard feelings between us. She was all spirit, a free soul. She was fully attentive and engaged with me. I threw myself into her lap and cried so deeply that she started to cry along with me in my dream as she held me tight and told me it was okay. She told me she would stay with me for three nights, and then she would leave. I was the happiest girl alive. I held her so tight, not wanting her to go. I wanted to tell her how much she had hurt me, causing agony throughout our lives together. I wanted to tell her she was the reason I had wanted to kill myself and how I struggled with all the pain and suffering in my heart. She held me close and asked me to go for a walk with her, ignoring all the voices and the crowds around us. I didn't know whether I should hate her or love her in that moment. I had waited my whole life to tell her what she had done to me, but instead all I felt was pure love. It was surreal. Nothing made any sense in my dream. It didn't matter how hard I tried; I couldn't be mad at her. The power of the love she was giving to me was so massive that I felt like I would explode. It was so loud that I woke to the sound of my own cries. I wept for the rest of the night. I was angry with myself. I had sworn that I would forget about her and live my life. I would not mention her name ever again, and I would be the hero of my own story. But she did something to me that I never felt in my conscious form. I recalled her face, the way she appeared deeply

13

concerned about me, and though she could not force me to feel anything, she was telling me that she would always be there for me.

But I didn't want that; I wanted to be angry at her. I wanted to live in my rage and resentment towards her for the rest of my life. I wanted to show others I could survive without the love of my parent, and that I didn't need her love to feel lovable. However, the truth was I loved those moments with her. It wasn't about parent/child love. It wasn't about the bond between the caregiver and care recipient. It was beyond physical form. As promised, she entered my dreams over the next two nights, and every time I tried to complain, she looked into my eyes in a way I had never experienced before.

On the third night, we were laughing and walking up and down the staircase together when she stopped me and told me it was time for her to go. I cried loudly and begged her to stay. I wanted to have more time with her. This was not the mother I had experienced throughout my life. Everything felt right and being with her made me realise what I had always wished to have – for us both to be free. Having no concern for mortal affairs, she was content and free of all her worldly damage. She told me I could watch as she departed from this world, and then she started singing a song to me. I remember I woke up looking for my phone to search the lyrics, and I soon discovered it was an actual song written for departed loved ones. She was telling me how she felt about leaving me in this world and that she left me with mountains, oceans, and sky. That wherever I looked, I would find her.

The next day, all I remember is listening to the song a thousand times and crying nonstop. I loved how I was feeling, but I missed her so badly. I was crying so hard that I suddenly found myself in the same exact place in the kitchen where I'd been when I heard the news of her passing. I felt my heart crack open. I didn't know how to stop it. It was out of my control. I needed to cry the whole day, to feel pure and vulnerable. Late that night, my husband became worried about this onset of despair, but I didn't know how to stop the grief from pouring out. When I forced myself to stop crying, I felt a big lump in my throat, so I replayed the song and let myself cry it all out. Later, I figured out I needed to cry to stop the pain. I washed my heart out with my tears. I felt so light, despite my swollen face and eyes, that I looked at myself in the mirror and burst out crying again.

I didn't want to go to sleep that night because I knew I must let her go. I saw her travel through a beautiful aurora-like gate. Another lady was accompanying my mother. I ran to the gate, and I begged my mum to take me with her. She smiled and told me I must stay. I begged the gatekeeper to let me go with my mum. She answered with a beautiful, heavenly voice that, as humans, we may only have three days in this world. One day we are born. One day we live. One day we die. I didn't want to listen to what she was telling me, and I tried to convince her to let me in. I looked back and saw my mother passing through the gate by way of a bridge that had no end. The other side was full of colourful aurora lights, and she walked over the bridge and disappeared into the lights. I wasn't there when my mum was born, but she took me on the journey to see how she became a light. It was magical. She looked so happy and calm, like she knew what was waiting for her. I watched her walk into the light as it glimmered brightly. By watching her go, we freed each other from pain and suffering. She wanted me to set her free, and in that moment, I realised how much I wanted her to be free as well.

The next morning, I went into the backyard, and she came to me again, this time as a butterfly flying about my head. She appears in different forms and shapes these days, but she hasn't left my sight since.

Part One

CHAPTER TWO

The Journey of Self-Awareness

My mother has gone to a better place. But how am I going to live with all the trauma and flashbacks? She is free. But how might I be freed from the emotional programming that was instilled in me over many years? It is not like you can just decide one night that nothing affected you and you become past-trauma free. Although I had been seeing my psychologist for a few years, and with her help I had progressed from being suicidal to reclaiming my power, I knew I still had a long way to go. I was diagnosed with Complex Post-Traumatic Stress Disorder (c-PTSD), and I have been going through extensive talk therapy and many sessions of Eye Movement Desensitization and Reprocessing (EMDR) in order to learn that my life is worth living on my own terms. After my mother passed, I saw my psychologist for a scheduled appointment. I told her about my insightful dreams and how I felt about my mother as a result. My therapist was very supportive and happy for me, and she told me that many people cannot forgive their parents after they die and that they also must undergo extensive counselling and therapy to overcome trauma.

My transformation while on this path has been amazing. I have learned that we can be angry and live with resentment towards those who have hurt us and left us to suffer, but they are no longer physically here to see this pain. We can choose to stay angry with their dead bodies, expecting them to heal us or take responsibility for what they have done, but their lifeless bodies have no sense or emotions. By keeping our minds open, we allow them to continue communicating with us in ways that may help us heal. It's up to us how much we want them back in our lives. During our time on earth, our lives are comprised of a myriad of feelings, our memories, and our perceptions of the things around us. When we leave this world, we leave behind our memories of the physical world and take our hearts with us.

A few months after my mother's passing, I was going through my podcasts, and I saw an interview between Jay Shetty and Dr. Joe Dispenza on the topic of "unlocking the unlimited power of your mind and healing yourself through thoughts". I still don't know why this interview popped up on my phone screen. I listened to the whole 1 hour, 21-minute interview and something clicked in my mind. After researching Dr. Joe, I bought all his books and listened to his programs all day, every day. It became my daily practice to listen to him and implement what he was suggesting. The main thing that stuck with me was how much sense it all made. He talked about the power of the mind and how we can change our entire lives by reprogramming our thoughts. His "quantum field theory" is about how we change the invisible field of energy waves that surround our bodies when we live with stress and trauma, and that when we react to the people and circumstances around us, we draw from this invisible field and change the waves of energy into matter. When this occurs, we live within a band of low frequency. Instead of living in waves of energy, we live in a stagnant field of matter and particles, and this leads us to continually force or try to predict outcomes. We no longer go with the flow. We hold on to our past and are afraid of the future. Even if we want to change, we still go back to old habits and the emotions behind past experiences, and we react similarly and predictably. The truth is that we haven't changed. We are just trying variations on the same thing and hoping for a different result. We are the same sad, bitter, angry people who wish things were different and struggle with the low frequency of life. Dr. Joe explains that we must be open to the unknown. We can do this by opening out hearts and ourselves to the higher energies.

I learned from his teachings that when we go around
feeling sorry for ourselves and feel or act like a victim,
we are casting those feelings into the energy field and
expanding our own suffering. He talks about how life is
about managing energy and where we place our
attention is where our energy goes. That's why I had no
energy for anything new and why I was repeating the
cycle of suffering. So, I completed all his twenty- to
ninety-minute meditations, determined to heal myself.
Let me tell you, it wasn't easy. Opening myself to the
quantum field, to the place where believing that all
possibilities exist in the present and creating a new life
neither based on my past nor trying to predict the
future, wasn't an easy task. I understood that
restructuring my life and changing my thoughts and
habits would require a lot of practice.

My entire life, I had been taught that others determined
my path for me and that I had no choice but to follow it.
Now I have learned to clear my mind and take
responsibility for it myself and to avoid the victim or
survivor mentality. I had to stop feeling pity for and
anger towards myself and stop pointing fingers at
others. I had to crack myself wide-open to let the light in
and cast out the darkness. I had to accept that things
happen for a reason and to take life as it comes. I was so
good at putting on my mask and pretending that I was
living my best life, but over time I had lost any sense of
self and didn't know who I was. All I knew was that I
had to go through the pain of transformation. I couldn't
avoid it. I couldn't go over or under or around it. It was
imperative that I go through it. It was scary and
frightening, not knowing what was waiting for me on
the other side. I had to rid myself of the burdens I
carried from trying to control the uncontrollable. I
started doing long meditations every night, and on some
nights my husband would join me. But I knew I must do
this for myself, that it was my road alone. I had to be

brave enough to go face it all by myself. There were times that I cried so hard that I could no longer feel anything. The experience was very strange, but I knew I had nothing to lose. I had wanted to end my life two years before, so I knew I could do this. *I had to do this.*

I kept listening to Dr. Joe's interviews and podcasts about his research. One time when we were in the car, my husband played one of his podcasts, and I memorized every word he said. Many months passed, and through meditation, I felt myself beginning to heal. I have had a few mystical moments where I experienced miracles and profound love. Once, while I was bent over putting the dishes in the dishwasher, I suddenly saw the whole universe rotating all together in balance and harmony. I saw myself in it, with the whole milky way and stars and galaxies. I could not believe what I was seeing. My eyes were not closed, and when I blinked a few times all I felt was a lightness—I was floaty and free. I walked through the hallway, but I could not feel my legs. Suddenly, it seemed my body was dissolving into tiny particles like atoms. I became one with the universe. After a few minutes of this, I ran into my husband's office and asked him to hug me as hard as he could. I was sobbing uncontrollably. After a few minutes, I told him what had happened, and as I had been experiencing a lot of these mystical moments, he knew he should not ask me any further questions until I came back to my physical form. Later, he asked me why I wanted to be hugged tightly this time. I told him I needed to feel grounded and present in my physical body because the power of the universe was way too strong.

As much as I loved the exhilarating feeling I experienced, I was also afraid. I was scared by the vastness. We are spiritual beings, and we are here to experience life in physical form and to bring consciousness to this dimension. It's a pity that we are so wrapped up in our emotions that we don't have time to discover who we really are. We are souls put upon this earth to have a physical experience, to get to know ourselves better, and to connect with our being. We are light and energy changed into forms to experience the different dimensions that we meet along the way to infinity. We begin as a light, take physical form to be born, live and die, and then change back to light. This is the process of our evolution. In the physical world, we need our bodies in order to evolve and become our higher selves. When we die, we change forms to continue living. We become eternal, infinite. Birth and death are just transformations from one form to another.

One of the many things that I have learned through my journey is that when we experience heartbreak, we erect concrete walls around our hearts. We try to protect ourselves from getting hurt over and over. We can't afford to let things go because if we forgive, we will forget what has happened to us. So, we shield ourselves with pieces of the past to protect ourselves. To remind us of the wrongs and traumas. While these things are true and did happen, we must remember that building those walls only ensures that we are the ones who block out the light. It's not that the light is not shining, it's that the wall of the past prevents us from feeling its warmth. I understand it is not easy to knock down the wall that we worked so hard to build, but when my mum died, I felt the wall around my heart crack open. My mind surrendered to the pain of losing my mum. I eventually realised that I would continue to suffer until I learned to surrender. My stubborn mind was addicted to victimising itself, feeding off the negative and low-vibration frequencies. I have always believed our minds can get us to wherever we want to go. However, I came to realise that they can be very destructive too. But the power of light is much stronger than we imagine. The light went straight into my heart, and I felt the warmth of the light after many years of blocking it out. It was scary, and I didn't know how I could protect myself from all the things happening around me, but I learned that I don't need walls around my heart to protect myself. I need more love.

My heart had waited for a long time to be released from the prison that I made for it in the belief I was protecting it, but it knew its way. My spiritual journey started after that. My mother's death was a new beginning for my healing. Before that, I was so angry and had so much resentment towards her that I never thought that one day I would be able to heal myself and help her heal too. I understand now that lingering feelings and emotions stopped me from being me. I had to learn to recycle my feelings and to grow healthy habits. I remember one morning after my meditation I fell back to sleep. In my dream, I was reading a quote that spoke of how energy can be changed into heat. In my dream, I saw myself as a giant standing atop two huge circular dimensions that were changing into wormholes. I could see everything so clearly. I saw my mother in a different form and shape. It was amazing to discover that while we feel broken and sad when we lose our loved ones, their eternity has just begun, and we are not separated from them. It's just the physical form that keeps us upon this earth, and we should wait for our time to come. There is no greater joy than knowing we will join them, finish our journey, and heal ourselves and everyone around us.

During my study of Dr. Joe's books and lectures, I came to understand that we are living in a parallel universe and that whatever we are doing here is happening simultaneously in another dimension. If we have an accident in this physical realm, it affects our vibration in the parallel universe but does not break our form. The accident happens in our physical sequence, not the core form of our being which is light and energy. Therefore, we can heal ourselves by paying attention and being aware of our connection to our core form, and then this energy will transform us in a parallel universe, allowing us to heal.

I had an amazing dream one night. In my dream, I went to a temple filled with brown-robed monks. They invited me to meditate with them. We started by drawing lotuses with our hands. It is said that the lotus is a symbol of meditation. It grows in a swamp and is a sign of stillness. While I sat separate from everyone else, each of us was holding a big bead in our left hand and a strange musical instrument in our right. I knew I couldn't play it, but I didn't mind. I was so happy and honoured to be among the monks. I started focusing on the bead and entered a meditative state. In the middle of my meditation, an old lady with a wrinkled face came to me and gently pressed her fingers under my eyes. She was wrapped in light, and it felt so magical to be in her presence.

After the meditation finished, I asked the Master if we could still come to meditate tomorrow even though it would be New Year's Day. He said that was fine. I said I would be coming, and a few others said they would too. I asked the Master what time we should be there. He replied, "9:99." I thought in my dream there is no 99 minutes in time, but I knew I would be there anyway. When I woke in the middle of the night, I figured he was directing me to the number nine. Later on, I looked it up and found many interpretations of what the number nine represents, but the one that made the most sense to me was that the number nine is the essence of creation and is the fulfillment of one cycle of life and preparing to initiate the next. I remember something came to me, and I picked up a pen and paper and start doing multiplication. I learned that the number nine repeats itself and that the cycle of life never ends or disappears. For instance, if we multiply 9x1 the answer is nine, and 9x2 is 18 and one plus eight equals nine again. If we continue doing the multiplication tables for the number nine, adding as before, the answers go back to the original nine. It is a cycle. I was certain, with all the things I was experiencing, that I was about to leave my old form behind and step into a new one.

A few months after that dream, I was introduced to the teachings of Master Thich Nhat Hanh, a Vietnamese Buddhist monk. When Master Hanh passed away, I watched the ceremony. I saw the lady from my dream who had pressed her fingers under my eyes. She was singing in the choir. Seeing the lady amongst the other monks in their brown robes made me realise she was a close follower of Master Hanh. According to multiverse theory, our universe is a result of consciousness. We know each other, even if we think we don't. We are from one source. *We are all one.*

Part Two

CHAPTER ONE

The Legacy of Suffering

Farzaneh Ghadirian

Whether we realise it or not, we must take off the veil that covers our eyes before we can see the truth. Not all aspects of suffering will be relatable. Maybe, you were born in a place with people who never experienced suffering. Maybe, those who were around you never let you feel what they feel. Maybe, they were brave enough not to show you what they went through, allowing you to believe there is no suffering in life. Maybe, you are fortunate enough not to feel what the rest of the people felt because suffering and pain are not something that you have experienced in your life. In that case, you would be the lucky one. For most of us, we are well versed in pain.

Eckhart Tolle continues to be someone who inspires me. In my studies, I was drawn to the way he explains how we suffer to learn to change our perception and evolve our awareness. How can we learn from suffering and change our views while all we know about our life is suffering? How can we change our perception and opinion about people or places while we are suffering? Those who are suffering are living at the core of pain and agony. All they know is suffering, even if they don't know they are suffering. They call it *living life*. When a person is suffering, all they reflect is the echo of pain. They teach their children to suffer and program a whole generation to follow. When we are suffering, we don't know how to evolve our awareness. We do not all wake up ready to learn and evolve. We wake and wallow and pass this on to those who learn from us.

Life is a path we follow. We laugh, dance, grow up, get married, and have children, all while we are suffering. That's all we know. We pass on this legacy to our children and grandchildren because all they see is suffering. If I constantly feel rejected, resentful, sad, or bitter, I am instilling these feelings in the next generation. If I suffer, then they too should suffer. We pass on what we know.

We are so deeply wounded by the emotional pains that no one can take it away from us. There are so many layers, and all are complicated and rotted and twisted in on each other. We avoid opening them up, as one-layer peels to expose to another layer. As each one is removed, we lose a layer of control. Why would we choose to feel vulnerable and unwanted again? How can we open those wounds up and let them free while knowing as soon as we put our guard down, someone will take advantage of it? Why would we do that to ourselves? We learn to protect ourselves, both internally and externally.

For me, after years of suffering, I learned to never let anyone in. Everything should stay where it is, where I feel safe and in control. My experiences taught me that this was the safest way. What's the point of having all these experiences if I don't learn anything from them? There must be a reason these things happened to me, and that was to teach me to close my heart. To not let anyone in. I took this lesson and became more aware. I am constantly watching. I make sure I never forget how and when past incidents happened to me, so that I may be able to defend myself this time if it comes.

I think many people can probably relate on some level. Perhaps they trust when they should not. Or maybe they feel like a burden in their own families. We sometimes are quick to blame our circumstances, how we were raised and treated. Perhaps they are still hurt or do not feel supported, or they feel trapped. There are so many things that can impact us.

As a survivor, I had to overcome what was instilled in me by learning. I am a product of where I was born and what I was taught. I didn't choose this family or my parents. They haven't chosen theirs either. They didn't know better than this. That's how they were raised. They have no education and were busy feeding hungry mouths. We must be grateful we are still alive. I understand they passed on their misery to me, but that's neither their fault nor mine. I can still wish they treated me better, that they were more responsible or saw me as who I was.

I must continue to learn from my suffering and change my perspective on life. I must constantly be more aware that there are so many people wishing to have my life. I should be happy with what I have, accept that suffering exists but is not the end. I can live with it, with those around me as they work through their own issues. I have lived through my parent's suffering and witnessed my children face their own struggles. I will not program them to follow only in my footsteps but will encourage them on their own paths. I am living this life for them, so that they may learn to stand up for themselves and stay strong and positive. I love my children and show them often. I will teach them to know their worth. I lead by example, talking to them honestly, shielding them when possible. I want them to know and understand that I do what I do to ensure a better future for them.

This is an endless road, the road of suffering. It is filled with ups and downs. We focus so much on improving the future that we forget to live in the present. We think we are living for our best moments, but those moments have already passed. We are so busy looking for the future to come that we miss out on what is in front of us. We cling to past suffering. We push for future happiness. But, what about the now? It took me a year after doing full-on meditation to realise the reason for my entire suffering is that I am dwelling too much on my past, on how I wish things had been different or what I could have changed. This behaviour is a disservice to the present I should be living.

There is a saying, believed by some, that suffering brings you closer to God. When I was younger, I thought this was the case, that my pain would only serve to strengthen my spiritual ties. I believed that those around me who suffered and prevailed, the victims of life, would be rewarded in the next. I was convinced that all my pain and suffering, my environment, was just preparing me. But as days passed, that better life never came, and I was getting more desperate. I did and tried every possible way to feel wanted and accepted by those around me. I let them take advantage of my love and kindness because I believed it was for the greater good. That I would be rewarded for my sacrifices. I lived in fear, stuck in my head. There was no connection with my heart. I didn't even know how I could make a connection with my heart. I thought the heart was just an organ for circulating and transferring oxygen and blood all around my body. I could carry on and complain about how the heart was not important for my spiritual journey. I realised no one before me throughout my family would know these things either. There was no place for feeling where I was raised. Feelings were not logical and rational. They were a sign of weakness. Too many emotions indicated I was not content with my suffering, and if I wanted to be closer to God, I must take my suffering without complaint. I was good at living in the past. And, in my eyes, the future was dictated by the past. There was no time for living in the now if I was focusing my energy on my past pain.

My mind became my enemy. All negative experiences I had faced left me blocked, judging those around me, creating an illusion I could not see through. I was so wrapped up in the bad things going on in my life that I became suicidal. I couldn't feel anything anymore. I couldn't understand why things happened to me. I was full of anger, resentment, and anxiety that I couldn't trust the future I was working for anymore. The more I tried, the more I felt like I was swimming in muddy water. I felt like I was barely holding my head above the water, weighed down and drowning in something I could not see. I knew I had everything I wanted but couldn't feel the pleasure in them. There was no joy or happiness, only pain and suffering.

I read different books and theories, slowly understanding how I was full of conditioned behaviors learned from those who came before me. I studied how their trauma became my trauma, their suffering transferred to me. I was raised to believe that part of my purpose was keeping them happy. But how could you keep someone happy who had never experienced happiness? I had trouble comprehending their reasons and methods. If they were looking for joy and happiness, why did it have to come at the cost of another's? If they were happy, why were they always complaining, sad, angry, and violent? They did what they wanted, seeking to fulfill a desire, but they were still not satisfied. There was so much sadness in their conditioned happiness. I knew I didn't want what they had, but I was so involved in my past that I didn't realise I kept repeating the same patterns over and over and expecting a different result. Looking at my life now, I never knew what I wanted even though I thought I did. Now I see that I didn't understand the magic of living in the present moment, living in now.

There are thousands of questions we ask ourselves every day. We struggle to find the answers we seek, weighed down by the emotional baggage of our past which prevents us from growing. We blame, judge, and shame one another. We struggle to relate. I came to learn the things that happened in my life in the past had to happen to make me who I am right now. I'm sure most of us have heard that things happen for a reason, but I never actually felt or lived in it until I started learning about Eckhart Tolle. His books and teachings opened my eyes to understanding why we live the way we live. We are so wrapped up in our feelings and emotions that we forget to live in the present moment. He helped me to realise that the most amazing gift we can give to ourselves and the people around us is to live with them in the moment. After all, one day we are born, and one day we die. Somewhere, between birth and death, is the moment where we live.

Part Two

CHAPTER TWO

Finding My Form

This entire book, particularly this chapter, is about my personal experiences. It is not the experience of my siblings, or even my parents or other family members. Everyone experiences their life in their own unique way. There is no right or wrong. It's all memories and feelings that separate us from each other. Having different perceptions of one incident or a situation is very common among us. We can't judge nor dismiss an individual's understanding from memory or events.

My mother didn't know there was a body being formed in her womb. Raising other children is enough of a distraction to not pay attention. Or perhaps an excuse to ignore it. She was struggling with a lot of unknowns and having another child was not going to help with that. She didn't need to give it much thought, knowing it would be best to terminate the pregnancy. My parents called the centre where abortions were performed and made an appointment. They both went. I was told it was early morning, and the place was not open when they arrived, so they drove to a friend's house nearby to wait. Despite worrying about being judged, my mother opened up about why she was there. They had a long conversation. Her friend convinced her that not only would aborting an unborn child be a sin but also keeping that child would be a better choice as that child would look after them when they got old. Something about her words made sense to my mother. After some consideration, she decided against going to the appointment. I was told by my mother on so many occasions that I was saved because of my mother's friend, and she knew when she got older, I would be there to look after her. My dad was happy that she had changed her mind. He wanted more children and did not want to go anyway. He was only doing so to support my mother. They both came back home, and I continued to grow in her belly, slowly taking form.

I was born into a big, crowded family. My dad was the
sole provider, which was customary in my culture.
Males were to work while mothers stayed at home and
cared for the household. My dad's own childhood was
cut short, as his father passed away before he was born.
His mother passed soon after. His brothers were older
than him, so they helped raise him along with the
community of mothers who ensured he had milk for
food. As soon as he was old enough, he started working
with his older brothers. My mum, on the other hand,
was the oldest daughter in her family. She mostly
helped her own mother to raise her siblings. My mum
had a good relationship with her dad, but I always felt
the distance between my mum and grandmother. My
grandmother was a caring and loving woman. She was
very intelligent and adept at learning. My mum had
very little education, and she mostly acted as the main
helper to her parents. She met my father at a young
age, and they were married. Soon after, they started
their own family. Life wasn't easy back then. They lived
in a rural area with all kinds of restrictions and a lack
of facilities. My parents managed to have four of their
children in that rural area. My dad worked for long
hours, and sometimes he was away from home for days
or months at a time. My mum spent her time looking
after young children.

Soon, they learned that living in a big city was a better
option for the family. After all, raising several children
at once was not an easy job, especially so far away from
town. My mother trained us to treat her with absolute
respect. We could not and would not share our opinions
or disagree with her. She had full dominion over our
lives, and my older siblings were responsible for looking
after those younger. I was raised with my older siblings
in a tiny apartment with a few bedrooms. It had a small
kitchen and a small bathroom. I remember the smell of
food coming out of that little kitchen and how

everything seemed so tall for my little body. I saw people coming and going to that apartment: friends, families, and relatives, though I do not remember their relation to us. My father would leave for work, and although I missed him, I learned to rely on my mother. That said, I couldn't feel the connection with her. I assumed she was tired, too busy looking after others or going out to do the shopping and all household chores. I would sit on the little window in the middle of the apartment, in a hallway staircase, and press my face onto the cold rusted metal bars waiting for my mum to turn down the corner of the street. I would wait with anxiety, crying constantly when she left. When I would see my mum walking towards the house, I felt relief and safety. This was probably because I was always in a state of confusion about what was going on around me. Living with adult siblings wasn't easy. I never knew what to expect which led me to be vigilant and cautious.

Eventually, it was noticed that I was not walking around like other children my age. They would walk, run, and jump, but I struggled to pull my body up. My legs would not move and felt heavy. It was tiring trying to move around. Something was wrong, but we didn't know what it was. I had come down with some sort of virus and developed serious symptoms. My dad came back from one of his work trips, and my parents took me to the specialist. I was diagnosed with Poliomyelitis. The doctor said that there was a possibility I could be paralysed for the rest of my life, but it was also possible that I would get better eventually. Time would tell my destiny. I remember seeing hope on my dad's face and worry on my mum's. At that time, I wanted to hug my mum and tell her I was going to be okay, but I couldn't. Even then, we seemed to have no problem yelling and fighting when angry, but we had not learned how to encourage and support one another. We would belittle each other and call each other names, but we never acknowledged one another in a positive light.

Despite everything that was going on around me, I always felt a warm light in my heart. Every day, I would practice pressing my hands onto the wall using it to steady my walking. I would watch my mum from the corner of my eyes, and she looked happy. But no one would come and support or encourage me. I knew that I must continue pushing if I did not want to accept my condition. So, I fought, determined to walk. I would hold on to the wall and practice every day. I would dream about walking every night. After months of repetition and diligence, my hard work paid off. I could walk. I felt a warm, powerful heat rush into my spine, and I stood on my feet. The joy of this achievement was beyond comprehension, and I knew then that I was capable of anything I put my mind to. I was only 3 or 4 years old at that time, but the power of that experience was profound. Somewhere along the way, I forgot about this, only to remember it later when working on this book.

By the age of 6 or 7, I started to have vivid and lucid dreams almost every night. I flew every night from one point to another. I flew right on the surface of the ocean while bending my legs down. I felt the coldness of water on the surface of the ocean and the cool breeze on my face, tempting me to get closer and closer to the ocean's surface. I loved my dreams. It often felt like a play date with myself away from everyone and everything. This was my secret place. I loved to go to sleep every night. I would see and feel strange things, a perfect escape as my mind processed everything I was going through.

It was customary for my family to travel in the summertime. My dad started a new job, so he didn't need to be away from us. I felt safer and more secure knowing he was home every night. I started to feel closer to him and loved him deeply. I wanted him near always. My dad was gentle and sincere. He loved all his children dearly, even if he had his moments with them. He loved my mother deeply, even if she didn't know how to love him back. When it was time, my family packed their trip suitcases and drove towards our destination. I loved leaving at night as I could sleep in my dad's big van and enjoy my dreams while being rocked by a driving car. I loved waking up to the smell of the ocean when dad was driving close to the shore.

But while on one trip, I had a feeling the good days would not last for long. It was either my fear or lack of safety from my young age or knowing about my future, but I often got bad vibes that I could not ignore. On one of those trips, my older sister and I went to find a public toilet. While I was waiting outside the restroom area for my sister to call me in, I experienced a vivid but mystical feeling. I was looking through the beautiful bushes of ferns around the restroom, and I felt something coming towards me. It was not a person or an animal, nor a hallucination. It felt as though I was getting drawn into something. I couldn't comprehend what was it, but I knew I had to let it be. I felt a warm feeling in my back while I was hypnotised by loops of four-dimensional space in the middle of the jungle. My connection got disrupted when my sister called me in. I held my sister's hand and refused to let go. My sister asked if I was alright, but I knew she would not understand. I couldn't describe it even if I tried. I knew there was a message in what I saw though. I was hit with lots of information that I couldn't comprehend. But I knew at that moment our family dynamic would change and that I would face lots of struggles in my life.

Another time, while I was on the bus stopped at the station, I looked out of the window and saw a little alley right in front of me. It expanded into a four-dimensional space leading me somewhere. The connection got interrupted when the bus start moving. I started to feel weird. I couldn't explain what I saw. I thought maybe I was hallucinating or daydreaming. I was getting older and living in an environment that forced me to be more like others, less 'strange'. I couldn't afford to be called the weird one, but I knew deep in my core that I was experiencing mystical moments, and they were full of joy and liberty. In those moments, there was no need for physical form, and that was pure freedom.

Part Two

CHAPTER THREE

Where Does Our Pain and Suffering Come From

It isn't always easy to determine the root of our issues. Going to a psychologist helped me to identify what was troubling me. It wasn't an easy road, but I am so grateful for finding someone to guide me. She always said it was me who made it happen, but I know, without her expertise and kindness, I wouldn't have gotten to where I am today. When I first started counseling, I was at my wits end. I had convinced myself I had done all I could do and that nothing worked. I was despondent and ready to end my life. I went to her office. I looked at her, observing the little room with a big desk and all papers and books on the shelf. I saw the chair in the corner right next to the small window. I remember trying to hide how nervous I was, not just about spilling my story to a stranger, but also being in this new space. She introduced herself and asked me some general questions. We spoke at length, over many sessions, and slowly I learned more about myself. I understood more about how I carried my pain. Her principles still resonate with me.

After many sessions and talking through things with her, I realised there are people around me who have a real love for me. I began to see how much I have to offer. I also saw how being wrapped up in my past experiences and identifying myself through the lens of the past kept me living in it. I did not hate the idea of contemplating my past, but my resistance to accept it left me constantly reliving it. Deep down, I knew I was too smart to let these past experiences continue to haunt me. I knew there must be a way to prevent myself from falling into the same destructive patterns over and over again. There had to be a way to relieve myself of some of the pain I carried.

I thought escape was my answer. I was tired of suffering due to my choices and the people who came and went in my life. But I didn't want to run away. I wanted to face my challenges, let them come to me, and deal with them head on. I considered myself a strong person, and I never let anything defeat me, whether that was learning to physically walk or to emotionally stand on my own two feet. I thought I was a survivor. But then it hit me. I wasn't facing them or fighting through them. I was resisting. I faced the challenge but did not overcome it. I ignored what I could until the next challenge came. Each battle had a lesson, but there was no acceptance or learning from it. I was defensive and full of excuses. I could not accept my circumstances, worrying too much over getting free from the chains of my environment. I felt like I was in the fighting ring. Is this adulthood or life? I was certain of one thing and that was, while I wanted to be a survivor, I was exhausted. There was no way I could face another challenge. I kept myself busy with work and school. I thought another degree may distract me, but I was tired of being busy. My life was unfulfilling. I had goals and dreams, but I was stuck. Living with desires was exhausting.

My life has been a journey. Being married and meeting different people greatly impacted me. Each of them carried their own suffering, different from mine. But it wasn't always easy for me to acknowledge that when I was so weighed down by my own. There are underlying layers of pain and suffering we all carry around in our life from our childhood and the way we have been raised, from the environment with our parents and siblings, and the painful memories of being bullied at school or being rejected by teachers and peers. Then, we get married, and we must live with that person's pain and suffering. Sometimes, we can't handle that. We may face divorce or single parenthood. We move through life constantly dealing with those who want to push us, being forced to do things that retraumtise us, interacting with those who attack our mental well-being. We face rejection, hate, bitterness, anger, and resentment, and it is hard not to want to escape. People tend to project how they feel onto others, but we must realise that this is not our story. It will not ease your pain push the weight of your worry onto someone else. But we tend to resist and push back against things that cause us discomfort.

This resistance begins at an early age. We are born into a family that we haven't chosen, and they may treat us unfairly or do things to us, so we learn to resist. We resist because that's not how we wanted to live. When a person grows up in a place where their ideas and opinions are not acknowledged, it causes them to feel unwanted. If they go to their place of work and are subjected to discrimination and bias, then this becomes another place they feel they don't belong. It all leads to resistance. This is not to say that these things are alright or that we shouldn't push back against it. But the constant resistance encourages resentment. It ignites the ego and fuels anger. This allows our minds to be the master of our body. We get caught in a cycle of fight or flight. We make ourselves into the victim instead of the survivor. When we become so defensive, we forget how to surrender to the process. We cling to the pain instead of letting it go. Our anger comes from a place of expectation. We expect people to treat us a certain way. We expect things to go a certain way. When this does not happen, resistance arises.

From the beginning, we think we are programming our minds to learn lessons based on our experiences, but still, we get stuck in a repeating cycle of suffering. The reason is that our life is rooted in resistance. We experience from a place of resistance. We live through the lens of resistance. We are all resisting something inside of us that has been shaped from early in life. It could be a minor incident, but it was specific enough that we became conditioned to resistance. We can pretend that we are fine, throwing ourselves into something new or letting the worry of others take the place of our own. Helping others is easier than sitting alone by ourselves and facing our inner demons. Seeing others in pain reminds us that we are not alone. It also gives us something to focus on. If we can help someone else with their pain or issues, if we do enough good, then perhaps we can avoid our own suffering. We seek happiness in anything that is not ourselves. We put so much distance between ourselves and our pain, that we can forget how to face it. We think running away from home (our inner self) is the only option, but the further we get, the more miserable we feel. These things will keep us happy for a few hours, days, or months. But eventually we will return, and it only becomes more difficult to face it.

Facing our suffering doesn't guarantee we won't be challenged by others. There is always something or someone who is bothering us, but it isn't easy for us to see past our pain. It always feels more extreme when it is your own. It is hard for us to forgive those who hurt us, so that pain lives in our minds, feeding our ego and ensuring that we can't move forward. Our ego encourages this thought process, forcing us to dwell on events from long ago, encouraging us to live in our pain. Those who live in a place of anger and resentment have been living for their ego. We might look like victims or survivors of our environment, but we are feeding our egos from the inside. Our ego is running our life and taking over the show. It tells us when and how to feel, ensures we keep our guard up, and leaves us wallowing in our misery.

We continue to suffer until those walls are cracked open. For me, there was a lot of buildup that led to that moment. I have since learned in my meditations that Zen mastery is all about facing our suffering and pushing through, replacing resistance with acceptance. My entire life I was resisting whatever I was seeing, feeling, and knowing. There was always something in my path. I told myself that if certain things were different, I would feel better. I couldn't see what was in front of me. I didn't feel right most of my life. I always felt I was born in the wrong place and wrong time.

When I was very young, there were often times that I felt overwhelmed or confused. I couldn't connect with others. I couldn't see myself fitting in where I lived. I was amused looking at everyone and seeing how they behaved. I struggled with interactions, always afraid of offending someone, unable to follow certain social cues. By the age of eight, I believed that I should have one purpose and that was to keep everyone happy. While I did not know what was going on, I could sense something was wrong and thought my job was to make things better. I would observe and absorb everything around me. Now, I know there was an unspoken pain and suffering being passed between us. There was always competition for love and affection. I didn't understand why these things were not given freely. It's just love. All everyone wanted was to be acknowledged. But even this came with conditions. The love that was given to them by my mother was entirely and firmly conditional. My mother would not give her love to anyone easily. There was no rhyme or reason to it. Being the youngest in a large family made it almost impossible to win her favor. My mother made everyone work and fight for her love, to prove they wanted it, to earn it. The others would try so hard to experience the feeling. Once received, they would do anything to have it again, even if it meant they got lost along the way. They neglected themselves, forgetting their own passions and desires. not knowing what they want in their life. However, to them, it was worth every tear, every drop of sweat, every sleepless night just to have the opportunity to bask in my mother's affections. I, on the other hand, was always asking why my mother didn't just automatically give them the love they desired. I wondered if she didn't know how. Maybe she didn't have that feeling either when she was growing up. Maybe she had it, but she didn't learn how to give it to others. Or maybe she just liked the attention. I started to believe that was the case, that she liked them fawning over her. If they needed her attention, they would not leave her. Perhaps her behaviour was an investment in her future. She had to condition them to get them to stay around her forever. When I was 8, I realised there was something that did not make sense about my mum. I knew at a very young age my mother was different. I knew I was not needy nor desperate. All I needed was a safe and nurturing environment. However, I also knew I had no voice in this, and no one would accept me as who I was. It is considered disrespectful when a child speaks poorly about her parent. A child is supposed be grateful that have a roof over their head and food on your table. I was told that my mother is a decent, loving, and gentle human being, and there was something wrong with me. My brothers and sisters did not complain. Was I the problem after all? This made me begin to doubt myself.

My dad, on the other hand, would easily give his love away to anyone who came into our life. He lived life to the fullest. He worked hard to provide for his family, He always took care of his wife, cared for his children, loved his family unconditionally. This is how I remember him. To my surprise, my dad never struggled to be around my mum. There were disagreements and arguments between them, but my dad let my mum be the main discipliner of their children, and he provided emotional support. He was the peacemaker. I remember every time my parents had arguments, dad would come home the next day with flowers, perfume, or a big smile on his face. While my mum criticised every decision, my dad would smile and nod and let my mum be right. It never crossed my mind that he was admitting he was wrong. I knew he did this to ensure there was peace in our home.

Because of this dichotomy between my parents, I often found myself gravitating towards my dad to get the safety and stability I needed as a young girl. Living in a big family was not always easy, but I still treasure the time I spent with my dad and the memories we made. My dad was so affectionate that everybody who met him loved him. They were drawn to his energy. My parents were opposites in that way, and I was so amazed to see two people so different raising their children together. From a young age, I always wanted to be related to my dad. I wanted to talk like him, walk like him, and be like him. I loved him so much, and I knew I would always be safe and protected with him by my side.

When I hit my teenage years, I focused more on planning my life and being a good student. For a while I wanted to become an actor. My family was busy living their lives. My oldest brothers and sisters were married now. The dynamic of the family was changing as more in-laws began living among us and grandchildren start showing up. I felt good about how I was progressing. I was an intellectual, clever, and determined person. I enjoyed spending time with my friends. I did get in trouble with the school principal quite a bit, but I always was excused because my school grades were above average. I was one of the top students in the school, and my teachers even let me lead class sometimes. I felt loved and adored by my friends. I even started dating a guy. We would spend time together after school. He took me to all kinds of new places. He spoiled me, and he got along well with my dad. They would sit and talk about different things. I loved that he respected my dad as much as I did. My dad knew that he and I were dating, but he never said anything. He

knew my mum would overreact. I was grateful for that.
I knew I could rely on him to always have my best
interest at heart.

But that could not last forever. Over the period of a few
months, my dad started feeling ill. He was not himself.
One day, it got worse. He was struggling to breathe.
Even taking small steps would leave him out of breath. I
would sometimes go with him to the doctor to see what
could be done. But it felt like the doctors were not
paying attention. I didn't know what to think. My dad
would struggle to even drive, but at only 14, I couldn't
help him. Things progressed. He wasn't the same. He
struggled with even the most basic of tasks. He couldn't
eat or sleep. Taking a shower would leave him
breathless. I would try to help where I could, taking a
brush and helping comb his hair while he caught his
breath. I just wanted to do what I could to make him
feel better.

He was not getting better though. I continued to do
what I could. School was still in session. There was a
program for actors at my school, and they were looking
for young talent. I was so excited. This was my dream. I
talked to the director and producer, and they thought I
would be great in one of the roles. I eagerly went home
to discuss it with my dad. I listened as my dad
explained to me that it was not going to be easy for me
to join the cast as we were in the religious minority in
my country. Because of this, I would not have the
chance to even make it to the first round of
performance. It hit me so hard. My dad spoke gently,
but he was still crushing my dream. He got up from his
spot on the couch and walked towards the bedroom. He
was out of breath just from this interaction, and he
turned back, looked at me, and said, "I am not going to
be around for long. From now on you have to discuss
things with your mum." I was even more distraught. I

didn't know what to do. What was he talking about?
Was he dying? How can I discuss things with mum? I
don't even know her. She doesn't know me either. I had
always had my dad to cover for me. To shield me. Mum
would never understand. She is always busy,
disconnected. She would never get my dreams of being
an actor or writer. Dad just went into his room while I
stood there. He got ready to go to the park with some
family. When they got back home, he sat in his spot on
the couch. He didn't look good. One hour later, he died
on the way to the hospital.

I remember when I got the news. I was at home, looking
after my little niece, when my cousin came over. I knew
there was something wrong. I pretended to be asleep. I
knew if he spoke, he would tell me my dad wasn't
coming home. I did not want to hear that my dad was
dead. I wanted all of this to be a nightmare. I wanted to
open my eyes and everything be back to normal. My life
was turned upside down. I prayed. I begged God to bring
him back. What is happening? I wanted to run out into
the street and scream. To beg for my dad to come back.
But I knew I couldn't do that. I had to put my own
shields in place and get ready because things were
about to change, and it would not be for the better.
A few days after my dad's passing, my mum started
lashing out. She was filled with rage. I had never seen
this side of her because I had always had my dad to
protect me. She was cruel, beating me to the point that I
could not breathe. One night, she hit me so hard that I
ran to the room, screaming from all the scratches and
the pain in my back. It burned badly. I was in so much
agony. I could not fathom why she was being this way.
What had I done? I remember my older sister came into
the room and told me to keep quiet and stay invisible. I
didn't know what I did wrong. I didn't do anything to
trigger her. It seemed just being near my mum set her
off, no matter what I did or said. I was constantly in

trouble, always agitated and scared in her presence. I did not want to be alone with her and hated when visitors would leave. They were a layer of protection I needed. I tried my best not to disrupt her, tiptoeing around her. I was ok as long as I was not alone with her. I think she knew if he continued behaving that way around others, they would begin to question it. But alone, the punishments were unimaginable, both physically and emotionally. I tried to follow my sister's advice. I wouldn't even breathe. I would just become as quiet and invisible as possible.

Soon, it was time for my family to move out of our family home. We could no longer afford to live there. My mum sold everything that reminded her of my dad, though she later regretted that decision. She was trying to minimise. We packed as little as possible. It was only me, my mum, and my brother going as the others had already moved by then. We were moving to a small rural area. My grandma and my sisters were always around, helping us prepare for the move. It was a few months after my dad passed and having people around helped my mother to live with ease. I know now that my mum was scared. She was afraid of the future, of how she was going to look after me and my brother, and she took all her anger out on me.

Eventually, it hit me that I was by myself. My dad was no longer there to look after me. My mum had just lost her husband. I had to know how to handle her pain and suffering. I had disconnected from her over the years, leaning on my dad. I no longer understood her, and I started to blame myself for that. I thought of myself as a selfish and egotistical person. Every time my mum mistreated me, I took it in because I felt guilty for avoiding her for years. I felt ashamed and believed that I deserved to be treated that way. This was my punishment for distancing myself from my mum. After all, my brothers and sisters got along with her, and she was not lashing out at them. It was just me that couldn't connect. It was me who didn't know how to connect with people. The family called me the "black sheep", and I had worn that badge with pride. I started to believe I was unlovable. And if I couldn't love myself, then why would my mum love me? I told myself this every time I was humiliated, accused, or attacked. Days passed by, and I started to get used to the behaviour. Deep down, I knew I was not loved by her. I was always in trouble, and no one could understand me. All the family members took her side. They did not want to anger her and face the same treatment. They reported every move I made. They rarely spent time with me. I was alone.

By the time I turned 17, I was constantly thinking of ways to leave. I thought if I got married early maybe I would get away from everything that was going on around me. One night, one of my relatives proposed and I instantly said yes without giving much thought to it. My sister quickly shared the news. I overheard my oldest brother was coming for a visit, and I knew instantly that I was in big trouble. My brother came in, and I ran to my sister's apartment next door to ours and pretended that I was looking after my niece. My mum and oldest brother walked into the room and told my niece to go out. They both started yelling at me. My mum was furious. I was confused. Someone proposed, and I said yes. I didn't know why they were angry. I was always treated like a burden, so I could get married, and my mum wouldn't have to deal with me anymore. Suddenly, I felt a cold sensation on my face. I was bleeding. My brother had hit me on the head so hard that the claw clip that was holding my long, curly hair on top of my head broke into pieces, piercing my scalp. I saw my little niece looking on with horror. She had come back to see what was going on. I looked at her and pretended I was fine. I knew my niece was scared, and it broke my heart to see her looking on in fear. After my mum and brother left the room, my niece came to me. I forgot about my pain and hugged her so hard. I stayed with her until her parents returned from a meeting. I hugged her, and I cried and cried and cried.

After that night, I was not allowed to leave the house for a month. I sat in a corner between the cabinet door and the sewing machine. I slept by curving into myself. I was not allowed to eat with others. When everyone was sleeping, I would sneak into the kitchen to find something to eat. They were no leftovers from the food everyone had so I would just grab something and sneak back to the corner. My brother-in-law and my sister would randomly walk into our apartment as the doors were always wide open, and sometimes they would make fun of me sitting in that corner. I could hear them whispering and laughing. They would call me a little rat, always moving around and making a sound like a mouse. I felt so humiliated that I wouldn't even raise my head to look at my little niece when she came to see why her auntie is sitting there and not playing with her. My mum would get angry with her granddaughter, telling her not to go near me. I tried to pretend that I didn't want to see her, hoping that would keep her safe. I was all alone again. It was just me against the rest of the world.

One day when I thought I was alone, I got up from the corner, went to the toilet, and went to the clothing rack to get a jacket to wear to keep myself warm during the night. Suddenly, something hit my head from behind. I turned back and saw my mum holding a long stick in her hand. She kept hitting me with that stick. She told me how embarrassed they felt by my decision and how ungrateful I was. My mum told me she wished I was dead instead of my dad and that I brought shame to my family. I whispered I wished the same. She told me to go back to that spot and not move from there. I was a 17-year-old girl on her menstrual cycle, feeling hungry and cold in her own home. I had not been at school for a month and was close to her exams. The school called my house and asked why I was not at school. I was a good student, and it wasn't like me to avoid going to school. My mum angrily replied that I might never go back to school and hung up the phone. I spent many hot days and cold nights sitting in that corner, hoping there was a light at the end of the tunnel. I wanted to go to school again. I wanted things to go back to normal. Every night, when the others were sleeping, I would grab the school bag I had hidden under the sewing machine and start studying. I taught myself different subjects. The days passed, and I was allowed to walk around or use the toilet and take a shower while others were not around. My grandfather was staying with us during that time. He had a hearing impairment, so he didn't know what was going on. The corner I was sitting in was out of sight but close enough to the main exit door that I would cover my face from my grandpa. I was so embarrassed to face him. Eventually, I learned to pretend that I was doing something, but my grandpa knew there was something wrong. He got tired of seeing me sitting in the corner all the time. I heard him scolding my mum for not letting me go to school, so she eventually let me go back to school.

My spirit was crushed by that experience. It was hard learning that no one in my family dared to question my mum's sense of judgment and authority. It was heartbreaking seeing how they behaved around me, but I knew one thing for sure. If it was any of my siblings in my position, I would have done anything in my power to protect them and defend them, even knowing the backlash it would cause. I never cared how my mum would react or how she deprived me of her love. It was important to me to stand up for what was right, and this experience only strengthened that viewpoint. I would never give up on them, on anyone in need. It was at that time I realised I am different. Not bad different, or good different, but still...different.

Part Two

CHAPTER FOUR

Ego Observer

Through my experience, I have learned that people with narcissistic personality disorder require our full attention. Those who feel strongly through ego need constant attention from their partner, children, and their friends and family members to feel superior to others. The reality is that they often don't see other people as people, but as tools. They are suffering from a deep pain body. They worry only about having others admire them. They don't like to be alone. They don't like to be told that they are not superior to others or that what they are doing is wrong. They are looking for fame, success, power, and recognition. They will program people around them to behave certain ways. If you are a truth speaker, they won't tolerate you. They will attempt to change you. They manipulate and mistreat others to sway them. They operate from a state of mind governed by ego, and they do not like to be contradicted. They are aware what they do and choose to be around people who are obedient to them or those who are naïve and easily swayed. They choose their partner this way and raise their children this way.

However, this awareness is not always conscious awareness. It is simply their being. Conscious awareness would mean that they are alert and adaptable. Those who live in the mind of the ego are rarely adaptable. The energy of people who are consciously aware cannot align with those who are constantly living in the state of the egoic mind. Narcissistic personality disorder leaves a person unconsciously tethered to the pain body. The children of narcissistic parents might understand that they are living in dreadful conditions and feel overwhelmed with the circumstances and programming they are subjected to, but they struggle feeling worthy and loved. The reason is that they have been programmed to feel like nobody cares, and their purpose must be to serve any commands given by the parent. Their opinions and ideas do not matter, leading to feelings of despondency and questioning their purpose. They often feel all the human qualities have been stripped away from them, leaving them as a possession not a person. This continues with them as they grow into adulthood where they make decisions based on the programming they received as children, repeating the same patterns that led them to feeling neglected and overwhelmed. Living with someone who operates from a place of ego causes lots of suffering and pain. It is hard to recognise, and we often find ourselves falling into the same relationship patterns as we lived in growing up. We attract what we know, and those with narcissistic traits will easily identify those who are malleable. So, we get married to a person who has similar characteristics to what we had earlier in our life. We are on the line of being used as a tool again without knowing it. Our life does not change, but instead, it continues on the same destructive path. By the time we finally recognise this, the pattern has already continued. We still feel worthless and doubt our purpose. Some people act upon it and leave the situation even if it takes them a while, but some people stay because it feels right to live this way.

Once we become prey to someone living in an unconscious ego state of mind, it is not easy to leave. It is hard to find a place where we are not treated as a tool anymore. The only way we can get help is to find the right psychological support, specifically help in dealing with past trauma. We must work on our personality traits and practice being conscious. Those who leave behind that kind of harsh programming know that they have been conditioned to feel and think in a certain way. These patterns of thinking could come from surviving a situation or being hypnotised to think a certain way by your parents or partner. Of course, it is easy to believe what we have been told, especially when we are younger. Our parents teach us to believe they are

superior and if anything goes wrong, we must look
inside to see what we have done wrong and take the
blame. By doing this, we are left to constantly question
our being. We become trapped in our minds. We don't
feel anything. We don't think anything besides what we
have been programmed to think. We are loyal soldiers
who will defend and protect the legacy that was given to
us. If we continue to live unconsciously, we will pass on
that legacy to our children. We will program them the
way we were programmed. The legacy continues,
generation after generation, and there is no way to get
out of the loop.

In some circumstances, life gives us more pain body to
learn to surrender. We are encouraged to not resist, to
determine for ourselves what is right or wrong. This is
how life teaches us to wake up. When we surrender to
the reality that we are living in and face the truth, we
understand why things are the way they are. We
become rebellious, doing and acting the opposite of how
we have been programmed. This is how we begin to live
free.

We carry pain within us consciously. We are aware that
our parents or partner treated us in a certain way, that
our past life was unbearable, that we are either victims
or survivors of our past life. We feel no one understands
us the way we want them to and that they don't know
the real us. Do you know the real you? Are we a set of
beliefs, craving an identity, hoping to escape our
predestined programming? Are we aware that we have
been living our life with a group of unconscious people
whose egos run their lives? Are we happy, truly happy,
where we are? Or, when we think about our past and
our parents and the family who mistreated us, do we
feel angry, resentful, and depressed? Do we want more
success, more money, and more recognition to show
them that we are not what they try to program us to be?

Are we aware that we are not aware? How much anger and sadness do we have to go through until we say enough is enough? Are we looking for a certain thing to happen to be able to move beyond our past? Are we looking for someone to come and free us from our pain and suffering? Is our internal happiness dependent on external reality? If yes, we are living in our egoic minds too. We might think we are better than those who raised us, but still the repetition of carrying past sufferings put us back in our egoic minds. We keep feeding our ego by wanting and desiring things to be different. We resist accepting that what happened to us was on a human level of the unconscious mind and those who did them to us didn't know any better. I know it's painful to accept that. We want to hold them accountable for what they have done to us. But to what extent? They are either dead or living like a dead person. Our obsessive thinking is the result of the conditions we have been raised in. We were left alone with our minds on the hardest and darkest days and nights. We think the only thing left for us is us and our minds. We believe that it is the right companion to have. It saves us from our trauma. It keeps us alive. We are here now but only because of our minds. The more we think that way, the more we feed our ego.

We must understand it wasn't our fault to be raised and formed in that way, but by continuing to only think about things we want or desire to have, we will get stuck in the loop of life. The only way out is to not feed the ego anymore. There was a time when we thought that the mind stays sane and saves us, but if we make more connections with our mind, the further we get from our heart. We should start bringing balance to our life by giving our hearts and minds the chance to live equally. Thinking that our heart is only an organ that listens to our brain means we never get the chance to experience the true power of a pure heart. If we surrender all our memories of sadness and betrayal, we give our hearts the opportunity for transformation. We need to trust ourselves and open our hearts to possibilities. We must start taking responsibility for our lives to gain the power to achieve our purpose.

I was tired of feeling trapped. During my marriage, my husband always assumed I would stay with him no matter what. He assumed I would never leave him. After all, it was my responsibility to serve him and live as I was told. My upbringing made me subservient in so many ways. I was a perfect tool for his ego, feeding is narcissism. I had no voice. I was formed that way, my life shaping me into someone who provides and cares for others. I was a perfect source of supplies. Everything was sucking the energy out of me, but I thought I still had something to offer. I couldn't give up on my children. I would fight for them. That's what I knew the best. To fight. Be a fighter and never give in to the truth. So, when the time came, I took my children and left.

For me, all of this meant a change was needed. I separated from my husband. I had never lived alone. There were always eyes looking at me wherever I go. When I was a young girl, I wasn't allowed to go out with my friends, and I always had to be home on time after work, no matter how heavy the traffic was. I always rushed things and was in a hurry. History repeats itself, and I lived with the same fear with my ex-husband. I was never allowed to go out with any friends, and he was always checking where I went and with whom. I felt isolated and constantly watched. Now, I was living on my own, watching over my two beautiful boys. I moved to a very tiny place. I bought a little bed for my boys and put some stuff together for the house. I enjoyed living there. I enjoyed the freedom I had. I finally found my happy place. No hitting, no head bashing, no arm twisting, no more black marks around my eyes. It was all me and my boys. Now, I could go out whenever I wanted and invite whomever I liked to my place. I enjoyed my freedom. I could raise my long arms to the sky and wear beautiful dresses and be comfortable in my body without needing to explain to anyone why I looked nice today. I could put the music on and dance like no one watching because there was no one to tell me that I needed a reason to be happy. I put my makeup on without needing to cover any black marks on my face. I looked at my big hazel eyes in the mirror and smiled at myself. I was free now. I would drive around the block and go in and out of the places without thinking about what time I needed to be home. All these basic freedoms felt so amazing, and I never again wanted to even think of giving my freedom away.

However, making changes in my life also caused some distancing from people I knew. My ex-husband caused me a lot of problems. He would not leave us alone. He acted like I was a possession, and he would not give up something belonging to him. He would have people follow me or knock on my door in the middle of the night. This led to increased anxiety, anger, and depression. Wherever I went, I felt like I was being watched. I didn't want to build connections with anyone because I did not feel safe with them. People who once knew me would gossip about me. I knew they were not my friends. I was free, but this came with a cost. My reputation took a hit. While that was unfortunate, I didn't really care because I was finally living for myself, and I loved that feeling.

It wasn't all bad though. My real friends supported, encouraged, and helped me to keep my sanity. I started to see a counselor and psychologist and attended groups known for supporting women in my situation. In those sessions, I would talk through my marriage and what had happened to me during those years. At the time, I was still confused about why those things had happened. It was difficult for me to trust anyone. I had horrifying nightmares about being chased by my ex or waking up still living with him. Sometimes, I would have nightmares about my children and their safety. I started to feel more depressed. I became bitter, and I lived in pain. I was angry at what happened to me all those years. My children would wake up crying in the middle of the night, screaming my name, telling me we must hide. They believed my ex was coming. I didn't know what to do. I was worried and tired, but I would not stop fighting. Confused, tired, and worried but still fighting, I reminded myself I had to save myself and my boys from this misery. I wouldn't let my ex traumatise us any further. I had to push through this and keep going. I wasn't going to give up. I had come too far for that.

I had multiple appointments every day: go to the police station and make a statement, go see a counselor to talk about my situation, ensure my boys had what they needed. One beautiful afternoon, after finishing my last appointment, I drove back home. Suddenly, it hit me that I am going back to my little unit, full of warmth and love. I was no longer returning to a cold, spiritless house. I rolled down the window, put my arm out to feel the breeze, and yelled, "I am free!" I couldn't believe it. But I was free.

While I was coming to terms with my positive changes, my older son was beginning to feel very anxious about all the court procedures. He was so overwhelmed that he couldn't go to school for two months. He was sleeping on the couch, crying, kicking, and screaming. One night, he opened his eyes, looked at me, and asked why I had not left earlier. I started to cry uncontrollably. I had no answer for him. I didn't know what to say. I wasn't even

sure anymore why I married him in the first place. I
watched my son suffering for two months, barely letting
him out of my sight for a second. I stood by him, hoping
that we could get through it together. I finally called the
helpline and got him a counselor. We got ready. He
threw up in the car on the way there. I waited for him in
the waiting room. I knew it would be difficult, but it was
important to me that both boys have someone to talk to
about everything. I wanted them to be okay. I was
barely able to look after my own mental health. But I
knew I had to help my boys. They became my main
priority. I would drive them from one place to another
and take them to catch up with their friends and pick
them up on some new homework. I was home-schooling
them for now. They couldn't go to school. Everything
was scary for them. They had been living in fear that
they would lose me at the hands of their father one day.
They were traumatised, tortured, and living in fear.
They still worried about what would happen if he found
us. I tried to answer all their questions every night and
assure them we would see the sunshine together when
morning came. Fear of the unknown was still chasing
me at night too, but I had to stay strong.

My children went back to school the next year. I started
going to university. I was working part-time, going to
the court, seeing psychologists, and answering millions
of emails every day. I was also looking after my boys,
showering them, feeding them, and reading them
bedtime stories. We settled into a routine.

Eventually, I decided I wanted to learn about human
behaviour, and I became interested in everything
happening around me. My psychologist helped me to see
the cycle that I was living in. The loop that others
created kept me occupied and confused. The more I was
perpetuated the cycle, the more lost I became. I had lost
myself completely and let everyone around me run my

life for me. I learned that I was chosen by my ex because he saw how my mother treated me. He saw what she got away with and knew I would be the same with him. I was caring, giving, and nurturing. He wanted to be served, cared for, and loved without doing anything in return. I learned the bitter truth. He saw me as someone he could use. I was raised to always put others first, to put myself last, to feed the ego of those around me. No matter how I felt, my priority was making sure everyone else was happy, often at the expense of my own.

It was hard for me to let the boys go to their fathers for visitation. When they were coming home, I would clean up their room and get the house ready for them. I picked them up from school, took them home, gave them clean clothes, fed them fresh fruits to eat, and helped them with homework. I cooked their favourite dinner and read bedtime stories to them. I would take them to their psychologist appointments the next day and go to their favourite places with them. I would do anything for them to feel safe and secure. Every time they came back from their father's house, they would be anxious, telling me all the nasty things their father had said about me. I knew I needed to protect them from that. It was not an easy road, but I kept fighting. It took six years, but I finally got full custody.

One day, before everything gets finalized, I received a phone call. It was a senior detective who was working on my case. I had never met the detective in person, but he seemed friendly and genuine over the phone. He told me that he read all fifty-three pages of my affidavit and was very disturbed by what I and my children had gone through. He had so much empathy towards me and mentioned that he hadn't seen a case like mine. He also told me that before they were able to get my ex-husband in for the interview, he hired one of the most expensive senior lawyers in the city. His lawyer wouldn't allow them to interview him. They couldn't press charges against him, but he wished me the best and advised me to hire an experienced lawyer. I hung up the phone, not knowing what to say or how to feel. I couldn't comprehend what was going on around me, but I knew I had a long way to go. I wiped my tears and embraced the disappointment. Just because he wouldn't be arrested and charged for all the pain and suffering he caused didn't mean that it never happened. I knew what happened to me and my children. I knew what we went through. I lived it every day for the last ten year. I realised that if he thought he needed to hire the most expensive lawyer in the city, it meant he wanted to cover up his crimes. As the detective said, just because he could afford to hire that lawyer didn't mean he was innocent. I told my side of the story. He would have the chance to tell his.

But I knew that his side was worse. He is an angry, impulsive person living in fear. His behaviour is destructive. His urge to control was predatory. Every day, he chose to torture me and never learned from his mistakes. He is the one suffering from pathological egocentricity, and he cannot love and is living in lies every day with his manipulative behaviour. The more I thought about those things, the more I remembered what my psychologist told me about people like him. I reminded myself I am not the victim of my past life and that I must start living life as a survivor. There was one thing that I couldn't understand at that time. Why me? Maybe it was all him seeing how my mother treated me. Maybe not having love from your parents was more common than I thought. Whatever it was, he believed he could prey on my good qualities. He believed he could manipulate me. He was still trying to have his way, even now.

I didn't know that psychopaths tend to go after people who have strong virtues and character traits.
Regardless of not knowing who I was, I figured I had to have good qualities if I could easily attract people. I have immense ambition that makes me the best in whatever I do. I have a competitive personality that encourages me to make things happen. Even though I have gone through so many embarrassing moments, I keep my head held high with confidence. I channel these qualities to tackle difficulties and solve problems in a forward-thinking manner. Those who know me know I demonstrate leadership traits, and they know taking on new responsibilities has never been a burden to me. I guess I owe these to my mother. She trained me to tackle battles and go forward no matter how I feel at that moment. She asked too much from me which made me ready for any difficult situation. Her love came with conditions which allowed me to prepare for disappointment, and her easy-to-anger personality caused me to always find a solution and have high problem-solving skills because I had to always watch and read signs before things happened. We might see the glass half empty at times, but the flipside is that the glass is also half full. What happens when we look back and see what we have learned? What skills have we developed? If I understood it right, there is a white dot in the black Yin which means in the darkest, coldest nights, we developed light and warm experiences that lead us towards self-awakening. This battle was another step in my awakening.

My cold, dark days and nights trained me to be able to make hard decisions and be ready to act fast while being logical about the situation. Having the courage to show one's talents does not always come naturally, but my mental fortitude is my greatest weapon. I am always loving and supportive toward my friends and family members. Even in the face of defeat, I will never waiver and will go on towards my set goals. This was a lesson I had to learn though. Early on, I focused on the negative sides and was always trying to find the answer to why I am the victim. I didn't feel sorry for myself, but I felt stupid and worthless in some of my decisions. It took me a while to learn that people use a combination of glib charm to feel the person out, tell them what they want to hear, and play the perfect match to their victim. Once the relationship is firmly established, they turn and slowly begin to devalue the victim, coldly discarding their emotions and feeling. This is gaslighting and manipulative and feeds their ego.

I quickly learned that if you are a 'high-pitch' quality person with strong emotional traits like empathy, kindness, strong conscience, willing to speak out, the people with 'low pitch' will be drawn to you because they know you will fulfil their endless desires. They want what you have. So, I started to be on guard to protect myself from getting hurt again. I looked out for traits like insincerity, manipulativeness, and glibness in others. I didn't want to be the victim anymore. I couldn't trust anyone. I knew I made a good target, so I had to be on the watch. Without realising it, I became bitter and angry. I started being harder on myself. I built up a cold wall around my heart. I had not paid any attention to my heart and lived in subconscious survival in order to protect myself. I didn't want anyone to believe they could get close enough to use me, and I started blaming everyone around me. I thought having all these positive qualities made me more vulnerable, a target for others to use and abuse. I started to squash all the good qualities that I had to offer, burying them deep inside. I was in a hidden war with myself every day and wasn't realising that I was the only one who gets hurt. I loved my children and did everything for them, but I didn't care about myself. I made myself busy with everyday responsibilities to escape the reality of facing the true me. Even if I wanted to, I couldn't. There was too much to handle. I went back to my old habits of serving, and I took on the role of taking care of my mother when she came to visit me in my small apartment. I would call and follow up on my mum's appointment with her doctors. I made sure she felt okay. When my siblings asked for support, either financially or emotionally, I made sure everyone around me had it. I believed that because I went through a lot, I had to help others not to feel pain and suffering. I knew I wouldn't hurt a fly, but I was a war with myself. I was emotionally and mentally wounded, just barely surviving every day of my life. I didn't want to love myself because I thought my inner self wasn't worth being saved. I was at war with myself because it felt better to live in survival mode and resist accepting what had happened to me. I wanted to see the world from my external reality and not have anything to do with my internal force. It felt better to be engaged with others and focused on them. Loving myself was just too hard to grasp. Accepting myself was just too hard. I didn't know I was repeating my old habits, that every day I was living my life based on the old sets of programs that I had. I had thought I was free. I could go wherever I wanted and do whatever I wanted. But this was just another escape method. I created a routine to escape myself. I was always running from one point to another, doing things and keeping busy. I knew if I stopped, I would crash. I was operating on autopilot. I did what I knew how to do: fight and flee.

Part Two

CHAPTER FIVE

Connection with Our Identity

Sometimes, there is nothing better than knowing that we are not the person we thought we were. In my case, I felt better after realising that I am not defined by my past or future. But I still had to ask myself why I felt so connected to it. From the time we are born, we are constrained by gender roles, our family dynamics, and the overall environment in which we are raised. For me personally, it was hard to reconcile that the environment I was living in was what would determine my future. From early childhood, I had wanted more. I wanted things beyond my control. I wanted parents who prioritized me and a healthy loving environment in which to grow and learn. When I was quite young, I deeply wished that I belonged to another family, even fantasizing that my "real", loving parents would one day come and find me. It was hard with such a large family, always so crowded and chaotic. I felt I didn't belong where I was, and I never connected with anyone around me. I was resistant from the beginning. Nothing felt right in that home. How hard could it have been for my parents to noticed that I didn't fit in with them? I was always trying to act different, talk different and be different. Nothing felt right to me, and I didn't understand why. Why couldn't I share one simple trait with any of them? Of course, they always had their guard up, sensing I was judging and disapproving of them. I am not saying I was either right or wrong. It was probably a bit of both. Many factors made me realise I didn't want to be where I was. That was the beginning my resistance and not wanting to live amongst them. While my siblings were trying to get my mother's love and attention, I was busy thinking about making a future where I wouldn't have to be compete for parental love. The more I resisted conforming to their expectations, the further my mother pushed me away. She wanted me to be like the others, begging for her love and affection, fulfilling her needs, and reassuring her that she was the best mother anyone could ever want. Fortunately, I found a way to differentiate myself from them. I drove myself to get good grades so that I could obtain a higher education. The more I learned and studied, the more distance I could put between us so they couldn't reach me even if they tried. My ego drove me to do my best every year just to prove to myself that I was not one of them. It still didn't matter--no one actually cared what I was doing. Using sophisticated language and having a title before your name could not separate me from my past and wouldn't give me a better identity for the future. Eventually, after working through the trauma, I had an epiphany: incessantly pushing myself to achieve a goal was my way of escaping the reality that was my life. I am not saying that anyone should tolerate a situation that is unbearable for them. We always have a choice. We can stay or leave, accept it or change it. Wishing things were different is either living in the past or in the future and avoiding being in the present moment.

We grow up with the decision to either be or not to be like the people we grow up with. Our identity is formed by what we see and how we think and act in response to that. We pick up habits that we might be unaware of, and when people around us point out those habits, we refuse to accept that we are acting like those who raised us. We don't trust our own judgment. We identify with others based on how we were formed or programmed. This is how we develop our sense of belonging. It is also how we connect. If we have been neglected, pushed away, or mistreated, we will build up resentments. These feelings impact how we act with those around us, and the more we do and deal with, the more our ego gets involved. Soon, we are driven by it. We think we know what we are doing, and we keep doing it and pushing through until we get what we wanted to prove to ourselves and others that we are more than what is out there. But when we get what we were aiming for, we feel like something is still missing. It could be higher education, a profession, a huge amount of money, a car, a dream house, or travelling all over place. There is never any satisfaction. We will never understand until we pause, allow ourselves to feel the pain and suffering, and invite the present moment into our life. We must go through the darkness of pain and suffering to break open and welcome transformation into our life. Going through humiliation, judgment, neglect and pain and suffering is the way to enlightenment. I understand it doesn't feel like an easy road, but we are living in pain and suffering anyway. Why don't we open the door and let the awareness walk in?

Eventually, some of us are lucky enough to move through the pain and suffering, and we learn to be open. We can't live in awareness until we acknowledge that in our daily lives, we are not always present. I don't mean everyday activities only. I'm referring to our unconscious actions. The modern life we are living causes us lots of stress, and it needs our full attention, but that is not the awareness of living in the present context. I do not recall if I ever knew how to live in the present moment. I don't think it's something that people practice daily. It feels better to live either in the past (wishing things had been a certain way) or in the future (desiring to achieve things). Who wants to live in the Now when there is trauma from the past to deal with or hopes to chase after in the future?

I believe that people are constantly avoiding or ignoring the present moment. There is never enough time to feel the now, and things keep changing and evolving around us. I didn't know how to live in the present moment at all. I was so weighed down with things that were happening around me that I didn't know how to stop and breathe. To me, it was just a waste of time. There were more important things to do instead than sitting and feeling the moment. I didn't know how to slow down. I didn't understand the concept of living in the now. People would tell me that I was always busy, but I understand now that I made myself busy because living in the present moment was way more painful than I could tolerate. I was constantly going from past to future and backward. Things must be done or dealt with that required my full attention. I thought I could handle whatever was thrown at me, and I did until I couldn't feel anything anymore. My physical body started to refuse to continue living like that, and my mental health started to deteriorate. I knew I had done something to myself, but I couldn't accept that I was the cause of it. I started feeling resentment and anger towards people around me and holding them responsible for the condition I was living in. I was blaming everything and everyone except myself. I didn't know living with that low-frequency energy would make me so miserable. I kept telling my loved ones that I was taking antidepressant tablets and seeing my psychologist frequently because of those who are acting out around me. If only they knew how to live their life or admit what they had done to me, I would be fine. I wouldn't need to take my tablets or even see my psychologist. I held others responsible. Now, I see I was predictable and unconscious. Something changed in me and slowly started knocking me down. I couldn't tolerate it anymore, so I started planning out my suicide attempt. That became my purpose in my day-to-day. I kept telling myself I couldn't change the people around me. I couldn't change the situation. But I could make sure they suffered too by leaving without me. The thought of killing myself became so strong that I openly discussed it with my loved ones. They didn't know what to do or say about it. It wasn't like they had training for this kind of situation. I didn't know how to disconnect myself from the emotions I was experiencing. Everything hurt, and nothing felt right. Thinking about what have happened in my life escalated the anxiety and depressive state I was in, and I kept wishing things were different.

I realised the older we get, the more resistance we get to our younger memories. If we are unhappy or grieving someone, we try to find a way to stop missing them by creating false memories to help us to cope with the situation. In some cases, if we have parents who didn't know how to deal with their emotions and feelings, they transferred the confusion to their children. We would be programmed to feel and think their way, or we resist becoming like them so much that we don't know who we are. Our ego finds the situation pleasant enough to feed the resentment that makes us believe that we are the victim of our life and that we must suffer to remind ourselves not to love again. Not being loved and mistrusting those who raised us is a good reason to avoid being fully present in our relationships and will cause us to choose people who are good at torturing us. Our mind creates a division between the phases of our life. There is a past, present, and future. We are disconnected from our present, and the only thing we know is our past that is connected to our future. We jump from being miserable and the victim to a person who is wounded enough to give his/herself the right to act out in any different situations. There may be people who are trying to support and understand us, but we will push them away. If we find a situation challenging or overwhelming, we act out and get angry, yell, or go silent as a punishment. We condition others to these behaviours, so they learn to avoid causing us more stress.

Some people live with their triggers. Everything, big or small, ticks them off. No one knows when the next attack will be or what will make them angry. There is no warning, and suddenly they are in a mood that causes people to either feel sorry for them or resent them. Those who struggle with this, our parents, siblings, partners, whoever they may be, come from a place of pain. They might not know that displaying anger and agitation is a way to numb the pain they are feeling every day. These feelings can be inherited from their parents and triggered by their environment or something they heard. Living in a place of pain is not something people would recognise in themselves. They are used to the way they are living, but they may be triggered in a way that is unbearable for them. There is always someone or something that makes them feel miserable. It's not their fault people don't appreciate or get along with them. It's either others' jealousy or stupid comments about them that make them unhappy. The blame always lies elsewhere. Living in a place of pain is not easy to recognize. Admitting that we are living in a place of pain might lead them to become resentful and angry with everything around them. The voice in their head makes them think that the world revolves around them and whatever that is happening around them is unfair. They become an individual that constantly feeds their own ego. In some of their patterns of programming, they became confused about their real self. They always have their guard up and identify everything around them with their ego. If they find themselves in a situation or with people who question their programmed identity, they become very angry. They are living in their mind all the time, and when things happen to them, they react defensively. They lack awareness. They let others' responses dictate their happiness. Their ego grows with each over-reaction. They think things always happen to them, and their mind manufactures stories that become real to them. They are always ready to be offended or angry about something or someone. The strong identity of the ego drives their entire sense of self.

Knowing this made me realise how my pain triggered my anxiety and how my fear of losing the identity of my ego triggered my insecurity. I see people acting like old me. They are living an unconscious life. It's so painful to watch them doing what I used to do. I was lost in fear, anxiety, and obsession, looking for validation and finding only loneliness. They show all the signs of living an unconscious life. I see the pain and suffering they are carrying with them. Our programming makes us lose track. It is a trap. Programs are a way to distract us from the inner self and chase delusional dreams or unhealthy habits.

It took me a while to realise that is okay to feel frustrated about things that are happening around me. It is okay to be upset when things happen that I have no control over. I now accept the small victory when I catch myself acting like my old self, getting triggered by something. By being aware of daily situations, I drive the vehicle of my being and get the ego to sit in the backseat. I feel love and grace in my heart, and I am no longer shaping emotions the way I expected them to be. I learned the universe has always had my back and is also helping me remember who I am. I am learning to allow myself to be me, to embrace it and take a responsibility for it, and then let it go. Complaining about it means I am resistant to accepting it as it is. As human beings, we hold on to our past or worry about the unknown future. We chase what we want, trying so hard to get things that are out of our reach. Imagine you are swimming in the water and don't know how to swim. If you try to grab at the water, there is nothing to grip. If you try to jump up and down, you will just continue to drown. When you stay still and flow with the water as it is and do not hope for what it should be, then you become part of the water and flow with it. If you don't want to drown, you must learn to stay still and float, allowing things to just be.

If we don't allow ourselves to be who we are, it is often because we have underlying expectations. Not accepting things as they are and resisting their form and reality does not change anything. But it may leave us filled with rage and despair. When we grow up with all the sets of expectations from our parents and caregivers and society, we dive into that illusion that things should be the way we want to avoid any insecurity or uncertainty in our life. We wish things were different and believe if they were, we would be better off. The illusion of changing things and wanting them the way we want comes from an unhealthy mindset that does not understand the fundamental procedure of reality. If we let go of the preconceived notions that things should be a certain way, and we embrace and nourish the true form of life, we will live in harmony with the universe.

I never knew what it felt like to be loved unconditionally. I only knew how to give love to those around me without fault, but I was not taught what it was to receive it. All my life I did what I could to keep and make everyone around me happy. I was so good at it. I loved and cared for others to the detriment of my own emotional well-being. Eventually, in the middle of the constant upheaval with my ex, I couldn't handle it anymore. I pretended I was fine. I knew nothing was right, but I still pushed myself hard, to the point that I felt numb. I was addicted to uncertainty, addicted to chaos. Everything took so much effort for me, even having a relationship with my own children. I didn't know how to fix things anymore. I kept fighting, seeing the lawyer, going to court, finishing my degree, working part-time to support my children, and not asking for any help from others. I didn't know how to ask for help, even if I wanted to. I was the one who always provides for others. Friends and family members would call me to ask about my opinions or recommendation or just for a shoulder to lean on. I just kept giving and giving. I didn't know my limits. I would let everyone push my boundaries further and further. Secretly, I hated the idea that I loved my family because of the way that they were always relying on me, yet I could not tell them no. I couldn't let them go either as I was afraid to end up being alone. My fear and anxiety were getting worse every day, and I didn't know what to do with them. Every night, I would go to my room, sit in front of my mirror, and cried my eyes out. I felt like something was tossing and turning in my stomach. I felt my heart shrinking. It felt like a lump was sitting in my throat. I didn't know what to do. I was dealing with too much. There was pressure from the community I was living in. There was the court procedures and my ex's daily drama. And then there was the positive. Along the way, I had found myself in a loving relationship. I was married now to the most caring guy anyone could imagine. To outsiders, I had it all. I was always elegant and confident. I had answers for any questions that arose. But inside, I didn't know how to handle them all. Having a loving and caring husband didn't take all my pain and suffering away. I did greatly appreciate his affections. I knew I deserved his love, and I gave it in return. But I had a tendency to self-sabotage with negative feelings. During this time, my new husband had a health scare. The doctors and psychologists could not figure it out. I would sit next to him and see his head start getting wobbly, and he would fall back to sleep. He had no control over his body. Some days, he couldn't get up from bed at all. I didn't know what to do. His parents didn't want me in his life in the first place. I was a divorced woman with two kids. In their eyes, I was responsible for everything and happening. I knew what I was signed up for though. I was attracted to a person who was loving and caring. He was drawn to me for the same reasons. So, it became the two of us living in a household, wounded and betrayed by those who raised us. There were so many times that we would team up to handle an unwanted situation together. We were always busy sorting out our families' dramas and problems. We thought we were helping our loved ones so that they would change, and they kept throwing their problems at our new and fresh life. Years passed, and my husband and I were still involved in family drama. We both loved each other so much, but we still didn't know when we would be free to live our own life. The more we were doing for others, the more we felt distant and separated from each other. The rush of living in that environment made us both feel more miserable every day. All we knew was something had drawn us to each other. We knew nothing happens on accident, and there is a reason we found each other. We loved to remind each other how we met and talk about all the experiences we've had together. We would discuss all the vibrations we felt and the positive energies we experienced while we were in each other's company, but as years passed all the negativity overloaded us from both sides. We started blaming each other for things that were going wrong in our life. There were nights that we would sit and talk about our past and were a shoulder for each other to cry on. We told each other how much we love one another, and we knew we would do anything for the other person to see them happy. It was just that we didn't know how to free ourselves from the loop of pain and suffering. We couldn't open up about our problems with anyone. Too many people relied on us to fix their problems, and others, we couldn't trust.

During this, I was still involved with the court process. My ex wouldn't leave me alone. He made all kinds of accusations about me and had been trying to ruin my reputation and painting himself as the innocent one. He went above and beyond in his efforts to get me in all sorts of trouble. While other people believed the father of my children's accusations, I was busy trying to fix all the physiological and emotional trauma he was causing to my children. After seeing my boys having nightmares every night, I found out what their father had been doing to them. My older son was a mess. He was angry, agitated, and scared. My younger child loved and adored his stepdad, but all the pressure from his father caused him so much anger and stress. This led them to having problems at school. They were not focused. The situation continued to escalate between me and my ex with our children in the middle. But finally, after many incidents that had happened to my children at the hand of their father, the court finalised the order, and I was able to have my children full custody.

With this, a new chapter of my life started. It was a time to undo all the trauma and suffering that my children went through. All I wanted was to them overcome what they went through. So, we all kept seeing our counselors and psychologists and continued our journey to healing.

Years passed, and we moved to a new house. Everything felt so good. It was time to make new memories. Before moving to the new place, my mum stayed with me and my family for a couple of months. She didn't feel good at all. She couldn't sleep during the night and only slept during the day hours. I took the boys to school every day and came home to stay with my mum while I worked on my final exams. One day, I looked at my mum while she was resting in my son's bed. She couldn't settle in. I called the doctors. I took her to all the good specialists I could find at private expense. I got her to eyes tested and her heart and all her other organs. No one could find anything wrong. They all said the same thing. She was as healthy as could be. I wondered if she was pretending or trying to get my attention. Then, I took her to a psychologist, and they said she is suffering from severe depression and anxiety. She was told to start taking pills for it, but she refused to take them. she didn't believe she was depressed or anxious. I talked through it with her and asked her to take them for a month. I told her if she didn't feel better, she could stop. One night, she woke screaming. I ran to her. I caught her on the way to my room, took her back to her bed, and told her that I would stay with her until she fell back to sleep. My mum agreed but couldn't sleep. She sat up and was gazing at the carpet. I asked her what was going on. She kept looking down, and she asked me if she was a bad person. I was shocked. I knew my mum always treated me differently, but I never looked at her as a bad person. I always thought there was something in me that my mum didn't like. I held her tight and pressed my face to her hair. I told her I loved her for who she was. I asked her why she thought that. She told me she was having nightmares, graphic and horrible images. I wanted to take her pain away. I wanted to talk to her about how things were when I was growing up, that I just wanted her to love me, or all that I went through since dad died. But I knew she was in no place to understand my pain. She was living in her own suffering; one she had known her whole life and couldn't let go. My mum was worn out from the collective pain she had been carrying. Nothing I could say would make her feel better. I asked her if there was anything I could do to make her happy. She looked at me and told me that she wanted to go back home. She knew she wasn't doing well. She wanted to die where dad was buried, in her country. She knew this would be difficult, as my eldest brother would not allow this to happen. But I promised her I would get her back home. She held my hand and rested her head on my shoulder and fell asleep. Regardless of my challenges with my brothers, I convinced everyone that she needed to go back home.

The boys were growing up and bust going to school. My husband and I were working and finishing renovating our new home. Life seemed peaceful. I had the boys at home with me. They were still seeing their psychologists, and they were progressing well at school. I was proud. Life was busy as usual, and we were planning for a better future. Neither I nor my husband wanted to talk about the past and the hidden pain we were carrying. We thought the harder we pushed the pain down, the sooner it would disappear from our lives. We didn't know we were driven by nervous, frantic energy. We were living in constant fear. Our entire life was pretending to be in control, keeping ourselves busy to avoid facing the pain. We were constantly running away from the painful truth. We thought, by helping others, we would feel like ourselves again. We were so wrapped up in serving others that we didn't know how to feel when we were on our own. We thought, by fixing people around us, they would finally leave us alone. We didn't know we were feeding others' egos. We made them feel like they could call on us anytime, without thought to our own needs. We didn't know how to prioritise our own needs. It was just an escape so that we could avoid facing our inner self. We knew going inwards would hurt so much that we tried to avoid it at all costs. The more we avoided, the more we hurt. We didn't know any better. So, we manifested the next challenge in our lives, trying to reconcile our differences with my husband's family. In doing so, we created only more suffering. The plan did not go well, and the outcome of that experience had me on my knees for the very last time.

Part Two

CHAPTER SIX

The Freedom of Living Control Free

I used to believe that if I constantly avoided thinking about things or stopped putting my life in order, I wouldn't be able to survive. Things must happen a certain way, otherwise I felt massive chaos in my environment. I know now that it was just in my head.

I remember once, I took my son to the family doctor to talk about the episodes he was experiencing. I was explaining to the doctor and was trying to make sense of my son's issues in my head too. I knew that every time that a specific subject gets brought up, the next day my child would feel anxious and start reacting. The normal smells around the house would make him feel nauseous. The connection between the subject and his body reaction was a reactive moment of past episodes he had. The doctor asked me if I was sure it was not in his head. It could be something triggering his reaction. I didn't reply, but it seems to me, as it is in his head, it is in my head. It is in everyone else's head.

The correlation between our past experiences and how we relive them when triggered is in our heads. The reality is that while it is not happening now, we still hold on to those emotions, so we keep getting triggered. I'm not saying getting rid of these episodes is easy, because it isn't. My point is that if we have no control over the things that happened to us, and there is nothing that we can do about them or any way to change them, our path to freedom comes from moving on. By thinking and rethinking and overthinking, we are trapped in the illusion of being in control, and we believe having control helps us manage our stress and anxiety. But you can also look at it this way. Not having control now may mean we have never had control, we never will, and it's all in our head. It's in our minds. The freedom of living control free is giving up on the idea that holding on tight to plans, ideas and the certain way things should be done. It is in knowing that we have no control, but trusting things happen for a reason. Things will happen to us whether we want them or not, and by being on guard constantly, we are simply living in a loop of stress and anxiety. We have never been in complete control, but we don't want to admit it.

Days and months passed, and I felt more confused every day. I was listening to podcasts, trying to find an answer or a reason for why these things kept happening to me. I was afraid and wasn't sure when the next attack would be or whom I could trust. The more I read books, the more I felt confused. Finally, I found something that talked about narcissistic personality disorder. I started reading more about it. I found more reliable resources and expanded my information about this kind of personality disorder. I started reading more and more on the subject. I knew there should be more books available, but I was so overwhelmed that it stopped me from understanding the concepts fully. After all, it wasn't just what had happened to me recently that had me searching for answers. I had a list of people I looked up to in some way, and they all showed different traits or exhibited symptoms. I read twenty-one books all together about narcissistic personality disorders. I read books about the neglected child, disarming the narcissist, or how to take your power back, but I couldn't understand why these things still happened to me. I have always been the type to dig deep for answers, and I wouldn't stop until I got results that satisfied my curiosity. But there was just one problem. I was opening all the wounds and revisiting all the trauma that I went through. I took all the packages out of the cabinets and now there was no space for more. I couldn't handle the load of them all. The more I tried to tidy them up, the more I realised that I have been stacking these traumas in my past, and that it could happen to me again in the future. I was suffering in my mind and my thoughts. I saw myself in the middle of a warzone. One happening within me. I felt so much physical pain, so much crushing pain in my heart that I couldn't endure it anymore. The truth was too overwhelming to tolerate.

When I realised that I have been programmed my whole life to have an identity that was not me, and that my childhood and adulthood were stripped away from me, I knew I could be the victim of a new strike anytime. I understood that I was conditioned to chaos, self-sabotage, worthlessness, and living in fear unless I was fulfilling a purpose. I was raised to serve and conditioned to think I have to serve to be loved. Now I have gotten the message. I am just a machine in a human body that was programmed to serve its purpose - keeping everyone happy around me while my identity and boundaries were stripped away from me. All I could think of was that I am not enough, my wishes and desires never got met, and the way I was programmed made me predisposed to put the needs of others before my own, regardless of how I felt. I was to give, to care, to love without thought to my own needs. I figured my life had been one lived in fear. Fear of failing, of not serving my purpose. And if this is how I was programmed, then what powers do I have in my own life? How can I get over a program that I lived with it whole my life? While I thought I was a human being with all my abilities, I am just a program. I am not running my life the way I wanted, but instead, my whole life was a sham, one lived to serve the goals of others.

I felt stuck. Finding my so-called identity became a huge dilemma for me. I wanted to move forward, but I couldn't. I felt my feet were stuck in the wet concrete, and I was sinking more every day. My anxiety and fear were winning. The uncertainty and the confusion around me were overwhelming. I kept getting triggered by my memories. I recognised that I kept myself busy my whole life to escape the truth. Being busy didn't mean I was in control. I was just causing distractions in my life because I thought I had a purpose to fulfill. I know now that my whole life was driven by my fears. My whole life was based on survival.

I also realised that my mum's collective pain caused so much negative energy that it formed an environment where she broadcasted her pain to us and now, we are broadcasting it to the next generation. Living with collective pain means that you are carrying the legacy of unresolved issues or trauma that our ancestors faced in their life. The legacy of pain is passed on to the next generation and so on. We become hypnotised to believe the standard pattern of living is the best that could be provided to us. We hold on to old habits and the traits of our caregivers so much that we will continue passing on the collective pain to our children and grandchildren in that matter. It starts making sense to me that the repetition of living in collective pain is not just history repeating itself. It's the way we get programmed that we have no control in our subconscious mind, and we follow what we believe is true. When we get programmed, we look for similar people. We seek to serve them and keep them happy. You do this in the line of duty and therefore, we fall into the same trap over and over. It's the same pattern but with different individuals.

I started on the path to getting to know who I was, but the harder I worked the more disappointed I got because my programs didn't support my wishes or desires. I didn't know anything more than the program I had. I didn't know how to feel free and liberated, and my subconscious mind kept attempting to put me straight back to what it knew, my old programs. I couldn't relate to anything else as my subconscious programs were based on limiting behaviour, self-sabotaging and disempowering. I didn't want to be limited anymore. I wanted to be free. I wanted to live the way I wanted but my program was controlling me with my subconscious mind.

Slowly, I started to have so many aha moments and find explanations for most of my questions, but the truth was devastating for me. Wherever I looked, I saw pain and suffering. I was in the darkest time of my life, and I couldn't comprehend any feelings. I saw myself as headed to the next challenge in my life, but I couldn't see the strength in myself to go through it. Back then, all I was doing was manifesting what was inside me, the pain and suffering. That's all I knew about myself. While I was living my day-by-day life and pretending things were going as planned, I was struggling inside. Some days, the feeling was too strong, and I felt I couldn't breathe anymore. I was gasping for air and the overbearing feeling in my stomach defeated me. There was only one option left to save me. The only way that I could avoid being the victim of this programming and end this suffering was to end my life.

I was thinking about it all the time, and I carefully planned my suicide strategy. I was going to end this misery, and the joy of thinking about it put me back in power. I had no desire to live and had no physical and mental energy to try. I couldn't look at what I had in front of me because I was too busy reliving my past every day. I was constantly worried that I would have a similar experience in the future. I had a long veil of pain and suffering from my past in front of my eyes that stopped me from feeling the love that the universe could offer me. Time was passing, and my darkness became stronger and deeper. I was in so much pain that I was slept on a couch for two months. Getting up to fix something to eat was too much effort. The emotional pain was so heavy that I couldn't feel any sensation in my hands and feet. If I fell asleep, I had nightmares, and when I was awake, my reality was a nightmare. Continuing to live in that condition didn't seem like a viable option to me anymore.

I struggled to find inner peace. I didn't know how to feel whole and overcome my programming. When I knew why my life was the way it was, I couldn't pretend I didn't know anymore. I knew it wasn't my choice where to be born. I couldn't change anyone in my life no matter how hard I tried. I read in the books that I shouldn't be the victim of my environment and how I had to rewrite my life story, but I didn't know how. There was so much pain to endure that I couldn't comprehend. I decided to write a letter to myself. I was going to tell myself how I wished my life was or what I wanted to do if I could choose. Suddenly, it hit me that if I was going to end my life, I would leave my children and my husband in unbearable pain. My children would experience the same pain I experienced after my dad's passing. This was the thought that woke me.

Thinking of how their life would be affected by my decision to end my life got me, I stood up from the couch, grabbed my phone, and started searching for a psychologist. I looked for a professional psychologist who dealt with childhood trauma, specifically experts in narcissistic personality behaviour. I called around, asking others for recommendations, but no one knew anyone in that field. So, I set to work myself and didn't give in. I knew I wanted a woman psychologist with many years of experience in childhood trauma. I knew I wanted someone versed in multiple types of therapy techniques. I figured I was looking for the impossible, but by some miracle, I found her. I read her biography before calling her office, happy to have found a clinical psychologist with interests in the areas of trauma and

PTSD, acute stress, anxiety, and depression. She also practiced Cognitive Behavioural Therapy, Acceptance and Commitment Therapy, Eye Movement Desensitisation and Reprocessing and many more. I thought to myself, I think I can trust her. She had the credentials I was looking for, and I had nothing to lose. At that point, every morning was met with dread and anxiety. I was seeing my general doctor once a week, trying to find out why I had no appetite, why I could not sleep, why I was so tired all the time. The general doctor doubled my depression meds and diagnosed me with severe anxiety and depression. I was at the end of the rope, so I called the centre, and to my surprise, there was a cancellation. I quickly agreed to an appointment.

Finally, the day that I was waiting for arrived. I was trying to prove to myself that I had done everything that I could and there was nothing left to be done. I went to her office. I started observing the little room with a big desk and all papers and books on the shelf. I looked at her chair in the right corner of the room. I didn't show it, but I was very nervous. She introduced herself and asked me some general questions. I was looking at her pen and paper and telling myself, here we go again, sitting in another psychologist's room and telling her about my life. Most of the ones I had seen in the past cried or felt sorry for me. I figured she would join the club in no time at all. I started talking, and she was taking notes and giving me all her attention. I told her about how I found out about narcissistic personality disorder, and I told her that I was planning to end my life. I didn't think at that time about how that may affect her, hearing me saying those words, but she listened carefully before speaking. She said, "I know you found all this information, and now you have unloaded all the stuff out of the cabinets and left them on the bench and don't know how to sort them out. I can help you to put them all back into the cabinet and close the door. You don't need to open the cabinet door again until you are ready." She continued, explain that nothing needs to be organised or kept neat and tidy. Things can simply be stored for a later time when I am ready to unpack them. Those who know me are aware that I prefer things in order. I always pay clear attention to everything around me, big or small. Her words were a revelation. Suddenly, I got a warm feeling in my heart, a feeling that I could indeed trust her, and this was very reassuring.

No matter how strong we think we are, there are times in our life we must let things go and let others help us. It's ok to be vulnerable. There is always someone who knows how to guide you. I have always believed something, or someone is protecting me, but I was coming to the realisation that the universe itself would always have my back. I was aware of the role of the environment in my upbringing but didn't learn about self-awareness or the impact of my thoughts on my life. I did not comprehend how I was broadcasting my thought in the environment that I was living. I knew there was an energy field beyond my understanding, and I was protected by it, but I couldn't see any connection between my physical life and the invisible realm.

I was very committed to seeing my psychologist regularly. I attended all my appointments and started to see the light at the end of the tunnel again. My psychologist gathered as much as information as she could, including performing all the standard psychological tests. She diagnosed me with c-PTSD. I knew that I would have to work to push through this, to overcome this disorder. After my appointment, I came back home and slept on the couch. This became my routine, along with updating my husband and my best friend about my sessions.

I knew I had to stop living the way I was living to prevent myself from broadcasting the painful trauma onto my children's life. The legacy of trauma and abuse had to stop with me. I learned I am more than my programming, and I must step up and take responsibility for my life. My happiness should not be dependent on external things in the outer world or how I was raised. When we live for others or external things, we cannot experience true satisfaction in our lives. Living in the survival cycle and surviving in a fight-and-flight response is not the purpose of our creation. We do not have any power to choose where we are born. We cannot change those around us no matter how hard we try, but we can choose not to be the victim of our environment. We can rewrite our own stories by practising, living, and being conscious. We change the world around us by creating what we desire. If we don't love ourselves and do not know ourselves, we never get to feel at peace. We don't know what it is to be whole again. After all, the purpose of the universe is to bring consciousness into this dimension. We have plenty of time and chances to make changes in our life.

I have learned a lot about my life. I figured out how much I was impacted by my dad's passing, which I never got to recover from, and how my childhood needs were not met. I realised how trauma taught me to close my heart and use only my head all the time. I have been living without really living. I was told by my psychologist that I have a highly resilient personality, and that I am very authentic about things happening around me. I agreed that the most difficult thing for me these days is to get up and get ready to face the challenges of the day, but I also acknowledged it is the most powerful thing to do. I wanted to find balance in my life but being programmed to live my life based on others' needs and desires wouldn't let me find that stability in my life. Lack of self-love was my biggest challenge.

I was advised to write a letter to my mum. I didn't need to share it. This was for me. So, I wrote her a letter explaining what had been happening in my life. I told her how much I have been suffering lately, how I feel disconnected from myself. I explained how I never feel safe growing up, so I tried so hard to create safety in my life but was failing. I told her that I now knew I am responsible for my feelings and emotions, that I had realised her abandonment and rejection during my childhood and adult life made me feel unwanted and prevented me to following my potential. I needed her to know that I never saw her as a good role model. That seeing her reject herself only made me want to distance myself from her. That she was never happy or proud of me, and it stuck with me. When my dad died, she was never were there for us kids, and she became needier, desperate for attention. This impacted me greatly, knowing that she had no true control of anything, so she tried to control us. I wrote about having to avoid my feelings in order to survive in her orbit. I had to create another version of myself just to exist and cope in that space. I held onto this false belief that I was responsible for everyone's happiness in my life, and this left me with wounds. I wanted to love myself to be able to love others, but I didn't know where to start. The way I was raised made me choose and attract a partner who exhibited the same traits as my mother, and yet I spent most of my younger years in this unhealthy relationship. I didn't get any love, and I was in constant fear of safety for myself and my children. I explained to my mom that both her and my partner left me feeling like I did not deserve to be loved. There was chaos in that marriage, I felt like I kept filling an unfillable hole. Now, I have a life that I had always dreamed of, but I feel so low and numb. The letter allowed me to finally purge these things which had been weighing on me.

The more I wrote my letter, the angrier I became. I liked the idea of blaming her. I felt empowered by shouldering my mum with the responsibility for everything that happened to me. It felt right to me. She did all these horrible things, and now she had to feel the weight of what happened to me. I left the letter in my drawer and wondered to myself if she would have understood it. I wondered if she would have empathy for me. Or if she would refuse to take responsibility for her wrongdoing. I doubted she would understand. She always had such a big ego that I doubted she would be able to put herself in my shoes, to feel the abandonment I felt when she herself had ever faced such rejection. I began to let my ego feed my sadness, and I started blaming others for things too. But the more time passed, the more obsessed I became with my past life with my mum. With blaming her for setting me up to fail. I held my mother liable for my past decisions and for being an example for my siblings, knowing we would all project what we learned from her onto our own lives.

Sometime after I began writing the letter, I heard from my oldest sister that my mum was not feeling well. I didn't want to talk to her because I knew I would instantly feel sorry for her. I was living on the edge, anxious and unsure how to look after myself, and talking to my mum would certainly not help the situation. I refused to call her, isolating myself away so that I could focus on my own healing. I knew I had to take care of myself before I could deal with anyone else's needs.

My psychologist told me it was time for me to do EMDR. When I expressed my hesitancy, she told me to trust the process. Hesitantly, I agreed. Going through EMDR wasn't easy for me. I had to revisit some of my more extreme traumatic memories. However, doing the EMDR with my psychologist, along with meditations and studying the work of those I find inspirational, has impacted my life positively. I listen to the programs and podcasts. I read most of their books and try to put their words into practice. I must be honest, some days staying committed to the journey isn't easy at all, but I push myself through it. I learned about Taoism, and I found bits of freedom and liberty within the pain and suffering. I understand now why I went through everything. The message was received. And that's how the journey of unlearning the destructive programming began.

Part Two

CHAPTER SEVEN

Life at Its Fullest

Farzaneh Ghadirian

Years after learning how to be liberated from my past
wounds and not be defined by the identity of
victimisation, my life has changed. I have moved from
being trapped in worthlessness, anger, and resentment
to being wrapped in love, joy, and acceptance. In the
process of self-healing, I went through three stages:
Physical care - eating healthy, exercising, taking
supplements, following a proper sleeping routine,
visiting my chiropractor regularly. My chiropractor has
expertise in Neuro Emotional Technique (NET). This is
a mind-body approach that focuses on the treatment of
stress related conditions. He uses this method for
patients who have neurological imbalances that are
associated with physiology and unresolved stress.
Emotional care - finding an expert psychologist
experienced in helping with trauma, surrounding myself
with people who truly care and support me in my path
Spiritual care - meditation, praying, connecting with
nature, Tai Chi, and attending spiritual services.

I learned that I had a strong bond with what I had
experienced in my past, and I was feeding my ego by
paying too much attention to my past trauma. My ego
was using my victimization, turning it into a power play
and keeping me stuck in the victim and blaming
identity.

Staying in the place of suffering, getting stuck in the
pain, was only exacerbating my wounds, and I couldn't
manifest the life I wanted because of it. Transformation
was out of reach for me. My wounds stayed open for a
long time, and this impacted everything around me due
to my constant attention to those wounds. But I learned
the hard way that I must close my wounds and start
healing my thoughts and my inner being.

Instead of putting my attention on how horrible my
experiences were, I power-play my ego and search for

the courage to deal with my injuries instead of living with them. Instead of being predictable and reacting to situations, I learn to pay attention to how I feel in unpredictable situations. Instead of wallowing in my bitterness, I focus on feeling worthy. I learn to forgive without letting my past trauma control my life. Forgiveness has been a big step in my healing journey. I fill myself with inward love and refuse to hold on to the hatred that was shaped by the wounds of the past trauma.

Feeling worthy and having inward love awakened my spirit. I began to enjoy the simple things: doing meditation, listening to heart-warming music, rediscovering nature, looking up to the sky, watching butterflies flapping their wings, listening to the sound of the ocean, and allowing rain to fall on my body. This had a profound impact. I also started following Buddhism teachings and Taoism and learned to be present in my life.

Self-knowledge has been the biggest lesson. When I get agitated and angry about different situations, I must stay in touch with my inward self and search within for what it is that bothers me. I embrace it with no judgment, and I stay present in the moment. I practice kindness towards myself and others to expand the peace within me. I learn to live in alignment with the energy of the universe and practice breathing in and out to bring forth harmony and balance into my existence. I understand how to respect myself and accept myself as who I am. I stop feeling pity for myself and become more loving toward myself. I embrace the whole of me. I don't need to ignore myself to be aware of others' feelings. I can change my priorities. I get to know myself and figure out what I want. I acknowledge that being different helped me get to where I am now. It is the darkness in me that showed me the light. It is the troubled side of me that inspires sanity. It is my deep humour that allows me to laugh at myself now. I wouldn't know this side of my life if I didn't go through everything that came before. I had to let things go so that better things could come.

Self-regulation, and following the course of nature, taught me that everything has a process. I learned to follow the path and not force anything or interfere with the progress of life. I accept things are meant to happen the way they do, whether I understand them or not. I let go of my attachment to memories and surrender to now. I sit with the power of stillness and become aware of silence, as it will guide me to live in the present. My soul knows how to heal itself, and I am guided by the universe.

I observe more judge less, practice self-love and not self-sabotage, focus on inner peace and not outer chaos. I have more faith and less fear. I sit in the now, being instead of doing. I recognise and embrace my emotions and have compassion toward myself and those whom I believe are the root cause of my anger. If I get triggered in a situation by my past trauma, I pursue empathy and understanding. I know that transformation will happen if I create a space for grace and love to enter.

These lessons continue to present themselves, and I embrace them. Such as when it was time for our family to get a puppy. My youngest child had been asking for a dog since he was a little boy. Life commitments and all the other stuff prevented us from getting a puppy sooner. We had rabbits and birds, but never a puppy.

We were all so excited, and I thought, after going through a year of the spiritual journey and healing myself, I am ready to take care of another creature. What could go wrong? I am meditating every day, writing my books, and educating myself fully about how to take care of a puppy. We have a huge, fenced backyard for a puppy to run around, and I believed we would be able give him the life he deserves. He could even be my meditation buddy.

I had everything planned out, and after months of looking for a breed that suited our expectations, we found one. I contacted the breeder, and as I was new to dog ownership, I put my trust in the universe when the breeder that he was going to send me a female puppy. I thought that was meant to be.

The day arrived, and we picked up the puppy from the airport. She was so tiny and unwell. She wasn't in a good health. My husband and I did everything to make her feel comfortable and at home. We had her crate with the teddy bear with a heartbeat and heat pack in it to remind her of her mother. She was constantly sick, so we bathed her and organised a time with the Vet to get her checked out. We knew we didn't get a healthy puppy, that the breeder sent us the one that no one wanted as they perused in person. Because she was in another state, we couldn't go and see her or other litters, and because we were recommended by a person in our state, we trusted the whole process. It was a mistake. I know that now, but I was shattered inside at what the breeder did to us. He was a well-known breeder, but he used our naivety and distance against us. Our new puppy had an extreme tendency to bite and nip. I knew it was a normal to experience some teething, but this wasn't normal biting. There were instanced where I had to go to the hospital. My husband's socks were always torn by her teeth. She was so extreme that I often found myself standing on the couch so she could not reach me, and my husband had marks on his arm where she had dug her teeth in deep and clung to him.

Days passed by, and I was furious with myself. Why I was so naïve to let the breeder decide for me which gender to have? To let me get away with not disclosing information about her temperament? My husband kept complaining, wondering what we are going to do about her, but regardless of all the issues, my son still loved her too much. We were at the point where we wanted to rehome her or leave her in a shelter for adaption. We paid a hefty price to adopt her, but our sanity was way more expensive than having her around. But, despite that having her was adding so much stress to our life, I kept telling my husband there must be a reason she is here. He still tried to convince me that I made a mistake buying her. I told my husband to give it a month. In that month, we would do everything we could to help our puppy be happy and healthy, and if she continued being like this, we would give her up for adoption.

I did lots of research about her anxiety and how effectively train her. We paid for puppy school, learning basic things that work for a calm and trainable puppy. We bought clickers and mouthguards and a specific leash, but we could not get her to calm down to trust humans. She was so vigilant and on guard all the time. Having a sensitive stomach only added to her anxiety, and I found myself often getting up in the middle of midnight to clean her and the crate up. I realised the food that was recommended by the breeder had lots of sugar, and she wasn't getting the right nutrients in her body. I searched and searched, and I changed one food to another. We did lots of home-cooking and worked so hard to find a solution to her sick tummy. It became a constant household conversation about what to feed her and how to do the training.

Meanwhile, I was still looking for the answer as to why she was in our life. I healed myself with regards to my past. We were in good financial terms, and I was happy with everything going on in our life. I thought the universe was helping me to heal better every day and showing me the path to freedom. But seemed like this little creature was ruining everything.

One day, I was looking on the internet, and I came across the line, "Your dog is your mirror. You get the dog you need, not the one you want!!!" Suddenly, something clicked for me. Do we have Coco because we need her in our lives? Is Coco my mirror. I went through that scenario over and over to make sense of it, but I knew I must let it be and accept it as is. I have always known that there are reasons that things happen. They happen for us, not to us. She came into our lives FOR us. What is the message then?

Time passed as I figured out that I have been guided by the universe. I understood that having my puppy at that time in my life helped me to come face to face with my vulnerability.

I learned there are more layers to healing in general. You must be attentive to the parts of you that you believed were not that important. That's why they say to sit with yourself, to be silent, and to live alone until you know you have completely healed yourself. With Coco, I had to learn to be silent and listen to something that cannot talk but has a very demanding personality. My puppy would help me to learn about the spiral of healing, to learn and practise breaking negative patterns in me. I realised the path of spiritual awakening is like a spiral. This meant, as I moved move forward and upward, I needed to revisit the situations or events that I was discouraged from confronting before. It could be my old patterns or behaviours or feelings that needed a resolution. After all, nothing ever goes away until we learn to sit with it and release it. We do this a little more each time we revisit it. Each time we spiral back around, we meet those unresolved emotions as they come back to confront us. We should not get discouraged by them. Instead, we must continue resolving them until we learn from them, and this will help us grow spiritually. We should not fight this or try to avoid it, even when we are tempted to fall back into old patterns. We have to remember that we are not the same people we used to be. We are reborn. We may be addressing the same issues, but we do so with new perspectives, sympathy, and a deeper understanding.

My emotional wound was still in me even though I thought it healed by forgiving my mother and loving myself deeply. The reality is...living with Coco taught me that I am still dealing with myself. She is a non-verbal creature that cannot speak, but the feeling I get from her is not her, it's how I feel about myself in that situation. It's in me. I continue to be the observer of what is happening inside me, and suddenly one day, I get how my mother felt when she was around me and I ignored her or didn't approve of her. Even not saying it out loud, my whole-body language and action were in rejection of her and all she was doing. I was showing her how imperfect she was. My perception of her was bothering her because I was telling her every day about how much I did not want to be like her by giving her only silence. It was my energy all along telling her she is unwanted. I wasn't brave enough to talk to her face about how much I disliked her, but my energy talked anyway. She knew her intelligent daughter was looking down on her. She knew all her other children loved and adored her, but I could see through her pain and wounds, and she wasn't ready for her pain to be seen, or to be defined by it. I always was silent around her, but she could read my body language. She was watching all my moves, and every move I made, every disapproval of her or turning my face from her, reminded her how unlovable she was. How hard it was for her to be her.

Rejecting the person who is already struggling only made her more frustrated. She would go around and talk negatively about me because she wanted approval and validation from others to counterbalance the rejection she received from me, her daughter. Nothing is more painful than being rejected. Deep in your core, you reject yourself and do not see yourself as worthy. She knew I was not like her other children. I did not seek her love and affection, because I did not believe she had it to give. We want our parents to love us but how can someone show us love when they don't have it inside them? She felt unlovable and rejected, which is why she was so bitter and angry most of the time. How could she give me pure love when she hadn't yet felt it? We can expect people to give us unconditional love, but some are only conditioned to love themselves.

This realization was part of me taking responsibility for my life. A part of having empathy and compassion for others. Seeing others as me. I'm not saying what she did was right, but I was knocking on a rusty door that needed lots and lots of grease to get lubricated. I couldn't give it to her, and she couldn't give it to me, and that's how resistance started. We were having friction with each other all those years. When there is friction between people, there is disagreement and argument between them constantly. You can give only what you have. When there is not enough love for yourself, you can't give any to others.

So, that was the grievance getting fed without me knowing it while dealing with Coco. Coco was under stress and did not want us around her, not because we were mean to her or didn't love her enough, but because we wanted her to be the perfect dog. We thought we were giving her everything, and she should be grateful for it. But we were not accepting her as she was. We needed to listen to her silence to be able to live peacefully around each other. We expected her to bring more love and joy into our lives, but she didn't experience a good life in the first ten weeks before we got her. We wanted her to enjoy what we are offering her while she was only used to living in survival mode all those weeks. No one paid attention to her. She was bred for the sake of a sale. She was not getting her mother's milk because she was so tiny and had to fight for her food which was only worsened by her stomach issues and her being a slow, fussy eater. She never experienced love. How can she love us back or even know what true love is while she was deprived of it?

Our parents are born for production. Carrying thousands of years of collective pain in their body and handing it to us as their children. They have been neglected, raged for, were unwanted and unloved, and we still demand that they give love to us. No wonder that when they do show they love us, it feels manufactured. It is a conditioned response. They are humans dealing with their pain and suffering. It does not matter how much we try to love them or understand them or support them, they are like an empty water well that we were trying but failing to fill up with our water buckets.

The way we have been raised by our parents and caregivers taught us to meet each other at the surface level. Those parents with heavy personalities live with a huge amount of pain and suffering inherited from their own parents, and that legacy of pain goes back thousands of years ago. Imagine your ancestors have been traumatised by an encounter, something that greatly impacted them. Now imagine that pain as a small stone or rock in your ancestors' pocket as they are the ones who carried it around with them everywhere. That pain is been passed on from generation to generation, adding more trauma with each generation.

Now add all those rocks or stones together and leave them in your pocket. Heavy, right? The burden we are carrying with us everywhere in our daily life is a thousand years of pain and suffering. If we add our drama, disappointment in our life and all the anger and resentment, to that of our parents, we pass on a dreadful amount of pain and suffering. It is no longer a small stone. It is a boulder.

The legacy of inherited pain and suffering given to us by our parents and the parents of their parents must be ended here and now. We must start our legacy. A legacy of healing and awakening. We have shared a lot of unpleasant past pain from generation to generation, and I believe it's up to us to transform others by owning our freedom. When we live in the absolute present and visit our parents, we don't need to refer to the past or even think about forgiving them. Healing our pain and wounds helps us stay present and not let our old patterns take us back to the past. Back to the path of suffering.

Grievances form into longstanding resentment and become food for our ego. Mine was a dark spot in me that I didn't know I was carrying. I thought I was fully healed but having Coco in my life proved to me that I have been avoiding paying attention to those dark spots within. Those dark spots had prevented my consciousness from fully rising. I thought I had forgiven my mother, and we healed each other, but I didn't know that I needed to forgive myself for the things I had done to her and feel how she felt when she was rejected and resented by me.

Without knowing it, I was feeding my ego. I was looking at it as a one-way street. My parent did the wrong things to me, and we have forgiven each other and healed ourselves, but the truth is I was not completely innocent. When I was only looking at my side of the story, it never occurred to me how I made my mother feel with my feeling towards her. We were healed together, but my ego was surviving on the hidden existence of my grievance. I struggled to find inner peace, become whole again, and overcome my programs. I would never know this if I haven't had my Coco.

I have realized, to have a meaningful, rich life, I must be in reach with the fullness of life. We have all heard about reincarnation and the philosophy of being reborn. I have always been fascinated by that concept and see myself as being reincarnated over and over. I finally understand the meaning of reincarnation. For me, it is all about understanding the past life and how we all are carrying a collective pain body that has been inherited by us from our parents and their parents thousands of years ago. We are all from one source, rays from one sun, and therefore, we are connected. Our parents are connected to this pain body, and so are we, and we are experiencing what they have experienced. Our mind or memory is the source of their memories, and we experience how they lived. The oneness of the human species causes us to experience what others experienced, over many lifetimes. It's not only how I lived but also the collective pain body of my ancestors that runs through me, causing me to live in the pain.

If we stop that legacy, enter the stage of awakening, and live with spiritual enlightenment, whether there is a reincarnation philosophy or not, we will have a peaceful and harmonious existence.

Acknowledgements

To my loving husband, Shamim Samimi:
Thank you for believing in me and supporting me.
Thank you for sensing my fears, my worries, and my
anxieties, often even before I do. I am so grateful that
you know me so well and always encourage me to keep
going. Thank you for all the wonderful conversations we
have and for just sitting and talking endlessly with me.
Most of all, thank you for teaching me what love is.

To my wonderful friend, Lisa Watson:
It had been a tough journey, but you have been there for
me unconditionally. I appreciate your advice and your
wisdom. Thanks for being an inspiration. Every time we
meet up, you guide me to the right path and get me
thinking of what I want to write about. Thank you for
all the laughs, cries, and sweet memories. I am forever
grateful for your friendship!

To the most accommodating editor,
Ashley Jane Aesthetics:
I'm very grateful to you for the thorough analysis of my
manuscript. Thank you very much for your assistance
with in improving it and for all you did to help. I am so
very thankful for your time and understanding
throughout this process. You are an amazing editor.

About the Author

Farzaneh Ghadirian migrated to Australia over twenty years ago. She enjoys reading books, and she wrote her own very first book when she was eight years old. She set up a library in her parents' storeroom. Farzaneh never thought that she would be a writer one day, but after years of self-healing and self-realisation, she returned to her childhood passion and began writing again. The purpose of this book is to show how she changed the legacy of pain and suffering inherited through her family line.

Farzaneh pursued her own spiritual awakening by following a spiritual path. She had lived many years at a low-frequency which led to reliving and repeating in a predictable line. While it was painfully comfortable, it did not promote growth. So she stepped into the unknown, escaping who she was and her previous programming in order to find her true inner self.

www.ingramcontent.com/pod-product-compliance
Lightning Source LLC
Chambersburg PA
CBHW051901090426
42811CB00003B/420